2019

CROSS PROGRAM
SUMMIT

**ACCELERATING GROWTH
ACROSS OUR BUSINESSES**

THE

COURAGE

TO GO

FORWARD

The Power of Micro Communities

By David Cordani and Dick Traum

NEW YORK

LONDON • NASHVILLE • MELBOURNE • VANCOUVER

The Courage to Go Forward

The Power of Microcommunities

Published in New York, New York, by Morgan James Publishing. Morgan James is a trademark of Morgan James, LLC. www.MorganJamesPublishing.com

The Morgan James Speakers Group can bring authors to your live event. For more information or to book an event visit The Morgan James Speakers Group at www.TheMorganJamesSpeakersGroup.com.

Interior images: Photography by Daniel Bryan: page 2. Photography by Christopher Churchill: page 22, 28, 38, 55, 56, 59, 60, 70, 73, 74, 77, 97 (top right), 103, 128, 138 and 142. Images courtesy of Cigna: page 31, 66, 84 and 108. Images courtesy of Sherry Cordani: page 11, 34, 140. Images courtesy of Dick Traum: 8, 15, 16, 19, 21, 27, 41, 47, 50, 52, 58, 96, 97 (top left), 114, 127 and 132. Image courtesy of Melissa Wilcox: page 44. Courtesy of Phelan M. Ebenhack: page 24, 25, 36, 100

Cover Photography: (top left and middle) by Christopher Churchill and (bottom right) courtesy of Luke Stackpoole

ISBN 9781642791600 hard cover
ISBN 9781642791617 eBook
Library of Congress Control Number: 2018907752

Cover and Interior Design by:
Anna Wingard, Katie Giattini and Victoria Apeland, Edelman Design

In an effort to support local communities, raise awareness and funds, Morgan James Publishing donates a percentage of all book sales for the life of each book to Habitat for Humanity Peninsula and Greater Williamsburg.

Get involved today! Visit
www.MorganJamesBuilds.com

This book is dedicated to all who set inspirational goals that many believe are impossible, and to those who give selflessly to support their journey.

CONTENTS

PROLOGUE

"Never confuse a single
defeat with a final defeat."

– F. Scott Fitzgerald

In the 1950s, the United States Air Force determined that planes with cockpits designed to accommodate "average-sized" pilots' statures were contributing to an increase in crashes, because the cockpits simply weren't the right size for the pilots. A surprising study of 4,000 Air Force pilots showed none of them had measurements that fell into the "average" category after all. Who knew?

Equipped with this information, the Air Force shifted to adjustable cockpits – adaptable to the needs of the individual – with great results.

This story sounds like it's about Air Force cockpits from a long time ago. It's actually about a very real and current challenge we see happening over and over again in today's world in different environments. We humans have largely designed our world for the masses rather than for individuals because we think it's the most efficient and least costly way to structure our communities, support systems and infrastructures. But it's not necessarily the best approach.

If you've ever squeezed yourself into a one-size-fits-all bus or subway seat that's incredibly uncomfortable, you've felt this reality intimately. But it also applies to profoundly important issues, such as the U.S. health-care system, which too frequently ignores each individual's highly personal needs.

This dilemma raises important questions. How can we do better? How can we complement programs designed for large populations with customized approaches that better respond to the unique needs and aspirations of each individual? How do we give individuals the support they need to achieve what's most important to them – whether it's better health, greater productivity or another personal goal?

Just as there's no one-size-fits-all solution that will enable you to overcome your personal career or life challenges (much as we all would love a silver bullet weight-loss or "get rich quick" solution), there's no single approach to solving broad societal challenges either. But we have seen time and again that small, passionate, tight-knit groups can come together – often organically – to fill gaps society simply cannot (or will not) fill on its own with its broad-brush approach.

These smaller micro communities, which we'll discuss at length, far more often than not benefit everyone involved – those who give their support as well as those who receive it.

This belief and how our experiences led us to it are what inspired us to write this book. Our objective? To demonstrate how micro communities, including partnerships between for-profit and nonprofit entities, can serve as powerful complements to societal programs and as vitally important adjuncts to what we can achieve on our own in so many circumstances in our lives.

As reference points, we'll borrow examples from the close, community-driven relationship between our two organizations (Cigna, a global health service company, and Achilles International, a nonprofit that enables people with all types of disabilities to participate in mainstream athletics). We'll reveal how our own micro community keeps the individual's needs front and center through services sponsored by national and international chapters of Achilles, including fun runs, programs and events for disabled veterans and others.

We are honored to have the opportunity to support and share in the journey with those who benefit from our initiatives and those committed to inspiring them, creating new programs that make a world of a difference. This "can-do" attitude perpetuates itself.

With this book, we intend to inspire you – and perhaps your organization or community – to make a resolution, define your vision and set a path to take action.

If you've ever wondered what you can do to help transform a person's life, this book is for you.

If you've ever wondered how things that feel impossible can become possible, this book is for you.

If you've ever wondered how – without having a large infrastructure or organization – single individuals are able to accomplish great things, this book is for you.

Throughout these pages, we aim to motivate you to help transform other people's lives. How? By supporting even one individual who aspires to achieve something they may not be able to achieve on their own. We've seen firsthand how doing this will also give your own life more meaning.

To get started, we outline how to form micro communities with like-minded people to empower individuals and highlight some of the incredible results we've seen people achieve.

The Courage to Go Forward shows how you can partner with others to take action and help those who most need inspiration and motivation to overcome obstacles and make their goals a reality.

A path emerges. The journey awaits.

The potential rewards are limitless.

Dick Traum and David Cordani

01

ABOUT
DAVID & DICK

Family and Persistence

The power of a well-meaning, extended community, connected by common beliefs and commitments, has certainly been a driving force in my life. My appreciation of a supportive community goes back to my youth.

When I was a young boy in Waterbury, Connecticut, my family lived with my paternal grandparents, so I grew up with the equivalent of two sets of parents. We were a close-knit family and I never wanted for anything. We also had nine relatives – aunts, uncles, cousins – living on our street, and we all looked out for each other. Everybody worried about everybody. And everybody took care of everybody. For me, the sense of community around the extended family unit was a part of my DNA.

That didn't make my teen years easy, though. I was never a great athlete, but I was always scrappy. I was the overweight kid (being overweight then wasn't as common among children as it is today). I was the last kid to make the basketball team, and even then, I spent most of my time sitting at the end of the bench. I stewed over that a bit. I wanted to be in the game and worked hard in practice to earn even a few minutes of playing time!

The experience taught me a lot about aspirational goal-setting, though as a boy, I certainly didn't call it that.

The truth is, I didn't like to sit at the end of the bench. I wanted more and I wanted to be better. Maybe this was the beginning of my ambition – both personal and professional. I just knew I did not want to sit on the sidelines – not there, not anywhere. So, I worked hard in practice to become a valuable player on the court, and my attitude was scratch, claw and get better every day. I made the team. And from there, whenever I achieved a goal, I set my sights on the next goal. I was always willing to ask for help from the talented and committed people around me, and I found that doing the hard work enabled me to reach my goal.

David Cordani at the
1999 Ironman Germany

David Cordani at the
1995 Ironman Hawaii

As the work began paying dividends, I embraced physical activity in a passionate way. I started running in college to lose weight, and I played a lot of intramural basketball. I lost weight, but I wound up injuring my knees. Well, that was discouraging – until one day, after several visits to the doctor, I watched the annual Hawaiian Ironman World Championship on television in which athletes swim 2.4 miles, bike 112 miles and run a marathon (26.2 miles) in that order and without a break. In a moment of what others may have seen as self-delusion, given my knees, I said, "I want to do that someday." Then, despite doctor's orders, I started running again.

One problem, though. In 1991, which happened to be the same year I joined Cigna, I couldn't even run a single mile. But I wanted to do better, and I recommitted myself. I started to build my distance capacity, running races, marathons and triathlons – first, at shorter distances referred to as "sprint triathlons," and then eventually, Olympic-scale triathlons. Three years later, when I was 28, I ran my first half-Ironman. Or tried to.

After an outstanding swim and a great bike ride, I under estimated the size and impact of the half-marathon distance that followed. Before I knew it, I was under hydrated and under nutritioned, and at mile four, with more than nine miles to go, I blew up in an epic way.

Total dehydration.

Total dysfunction.

Then I pulled off one of the dumbest stunts ever known to Iron-mankind.

I walked into the woods, found a patch of grass and fell asleep (yes, you read that right), arguably the worst thing to do when you're dehydrated, dysfunctional and losing your sensibilities. Fortunately, I woke up, got back onto the course, and walked – turning a 4:45 estimated finish time into a six-hour journey. Bent over with exhaustion, I said to myself, "I will never compete in another half-Ironman. And the Ironman? Total pipe dream."

By the time I drove the three painful hours home, I had sorted through the things I had done wrong. I underestimated the magnitude of the event. I didn't ask other competitors for their help or insights in my practice and preparation. And when all the signals were screaming at me to adjust along the way, I missed every one of them. I blew through all the indicators.

Others would later explain how the heat and humidity caused my body to act differently than it did normally, and they told me about the importance of hydration and nutrition en route. (I still think that's the most underestimated part of any endurance event.)

This setback – my greatest failure among the well-in-excess of 125 triathlons I've ever attempted – became my best learning. I had to do better. With the support of other triathletes, I prepared again. I finally completed a half-Ironman less than one year later, and went on to complete the Hawaiian Ironman in 1995 – the very race that motivated me to get off my couch.

Of note is that in Hawaii, I saw athletes who were in far superior condition, curled up in a ball on the roadside and in the lava fields. Dehydration, lack of nutrition: I had seen that before!

These were crucial lessons – ones I continue to return to time and again. When I work with athletes today, I teach them about the importance of having a community and extended family around you, watching for signals that you need help, and making adjustments and keeping your eyes open for indicators along the way.

As I look back, I had set a goal even though one could argue I had no "right" to set such a high goal. You see, I had never been an accomplished swimmer, cyclist or distance runner. There was no rationale that supported why my attempt at my first half-Ironman could possibly be successful. I realized how falling short of a goal can be a harsh reminder of the value of having a solid plan in place that enables you to get there.

Fortunately I was surrounded by a supportive community of like-minded people who strengthened my resolve. Failure under those circumstances would never be an option. So, building and maintaining a foundational community – the family dynamic, whether through blood relatives or "acquired" family – have always been foremost in my mind.

Achievement, Spirit and the Joy of Giving

I've witnessed that 'special sauce' that compels people to act. It's the feeling of self-actualization that drives our achievements. I've seen mountain climbers forging a crevasse to conquer a summit and Ironman participants drawing from every last ounce of energy to reach the finish line. I strongly believe we all have an innate instinct – a quiet, internal voice – that speaks to us, and drives us. I think of it as our spirit.

My own spirit of achievement started very early. At age three, I built a great giant block building. Later I collected the largest number of books for donations at Hunter College Elementary School in New York. By my early teens, I had earned the Most Valuable Player track and field award in a seventh- and eighth-grade competition and medaled as a ninth-grader in a high school wrestling tournament.

Perhaps the largest jolt came in my junior year at the Horace Mann School in New York when I wrestled a world-class competitor who had placed in the Olympic trials the year before. After being taken down and almost pinned during the first period, I bridged and turned him over on his back. This was my greatest physical effort ever, and I was amazed that this world-class athlete was almost helpless on his back. The crowd was screaming and cheering for me from the sidelines – something I had never experienced before. What a buzz! On the school spirit scale, this was a 10.

The first period was over and the referee never called it a pin, although even today I recall that many sitting in the stands thought he should have. I ultimately lost the match to a better opponent, but I felt like a hero.

Dick Traum riding handcycle

Dick Traum speaking
at Achilles event

That was one example of a key lesson I've learned about myself throughout my life. First, I really enjoy achieving. I associate success with the affection I receive from it. Moreover, at a very young age when I collected those books for donation, I learned about the joy of giving. Again, I associate it with the positive interactions that resulted.

This was, perhaps, the genesis of how David McClelland's theory of needs influenced my life. A famed American 20th-century psychologist, McClelland spent much of his career working on his acquired-needs theory, and how our needs are shaped by our lifetime experiences. McClelland classified our needs into three categories: achievement, affiliation and power. For me, at an early age, the need to achieve was clearly a driving force in my life.

But life sometimes has other plans for us.

Dick and Betsy Traum on wedding day

Dick Traum becomes first amputee to finish 100km ultra-event, Poland, 1980s

We all have a road-not-taken tale to tell, and sometimes we have no control over the storyline. When I was 24, my fiancée and I drove out of New York to meet her friends in Philadelphia. I remember it well: Sunday, May 30, 1965. Memorial Day weekend. On the spur of the moment, we decided to stop for gas on the New Jersey Turnpike near Camden, N.J., rather than wait until we reached Philadelphia. In the words of Robert Frost, that has made all the difference.

My fiancée went to the ladies' room and I stood behind the car while it was getting fueled. A second car pulled up behind me and as the driver tried to open his right front door, it became stuck. His car, still in drive, began moving toward me. The driver slammed on the pedal. But it was the gas pedal instead of the brake. He hit me so hard that the impact broke the radiator on his Chrysler and moved my car, which was in park, several feet. Six days later, my crushed right leg was amputated above the knee. My left leg and my life were saved. The surgeon told me that I was dead for about 30 seconds. He also said that if I had been over 40, I would not have survived.

But I did survive and learned a great lesson at age 24: Life isn't forever. During my rehabilitation period, I had lots of time to think. I recall a man's life expectancy was around 73 years. So, in theory, at 24, roughly one-third of my life already had passed.

If you consider the 73 years a male of my generation was expected to live, my first third comprised preschool, elementary school, high school, college and graduate school. These were the learning years.

The second third was largely committed to business: Young professional, consultant, small-business supervisor and small-business manager.

For the final third, beginning at age 43, I've spent most of my time with Achilles International – gradually escalating my involvement from part time to full time, and from supervisor to manager.

Fortunately, I passed 73 several years ago! And I honestly believe I have three reasons to thank for that: my involvement with Achilles, my embrace of the micro communities referenced in the prologue and my commitment to achievement.

> Looking back, the jolts of spirit I experienced and my drive to achieve only escalated after being introduced to running as an amputee.

I remember finishing my first marathon in 1976. The shouts and applause during the final quarter mile were similar to those of a football player running for a touchdown, except they lasted for the several minutes it took me to reach the finish line.

At the closing awards ceremony in Lincoln Center in New York, I was presented with a special award for being the first amputee to run a marathon. A huge group stood up and kept applauding for me. I motioned to the crowd, "Enough, please sit down."

But I loved it! It energized me beyond words and caused me to start thinking ahead to my next accomplishments even before the applause died down. This is spirit. This is the reinforcement that encourages achievement.

As I progressed in my journey of achievement, a different aspect of spirit became evident to me. It was the joy of generating a jolt for others – of helping others benefit from the same support I had been lucky enough to receive.

In my mind, I had graduated from the child who receives affection to the adult who understands the enormous power of giving affection. There is a great joy in seeing others succeed because I have moved from being the child – the high-school kid who runs a race – to being the adult who watches my kids doing the race. It's even more fun cheering on those whom you have worked with than it is doing it yourself. Certainly after you've done a few yourself, you love seeing others succeed.

The power of this dynamic became apparent in 1981 when I was invited to participate in fundraising activities and races after the death of Terry Fox. Terry had lost his leg to cancer at age 17 and went on to inspire others when he ran more than 3,300 miles across his native Canada to raise awareness for cancer research. He died one month before his 23rd birthday, after his cancer returned.

From that experience and others, I found that helping other people became as big a buzz for me as receiving recognition. This concept of joy from helping eventually generated the idea of an eight-week course on running, which evolved into an international phenomenon.

I needed to act on this!

And so, Achilles International was created in January 1983, with scheduled workouts on Wednesday evenings and Saturday mornings in New York. You need to understand the world was different in the early 1980s. Running wasn't a big sport for people with disabilities. Who would consider coming out on a dark, cold winter evening to run in what was, at that time, a dangerous Central Park? Not many. My fear as the founder was that I would come to a workout, have no one show up and want to hide.

It almost – but never – happened. One night, my friend Linda Down, who has cerebral palsy and uses crutches, was a bit late, but when she showed, the two of us ran together. Then things improved. I would pick up children at Ronald McDonald House who were undergoing chemotherapy, drive them to the workout and drop them off when we were done. We would cover subway fare for those who could not afford the trip. Whatever was necessary, we did. It worked.

Spring arrived, and the park was light and warm. More people began participating. We were on our way.

First group Achilles photo, 1983

Dick Traum with Achilles handcyclists

In Dick's Words: The Power of Partnership

I've learned a lot, too, from working with David and seeing what we can achieve together. At Cigna, David oversees more than 95 million customer relationships in 30-plus countries. In this work, he witnesses his team helping people lead healthier, more productive lives; the Cigna team provides individualized support that often draws on the power of community partnerships. And in his personal life as a veteran of more than 125 triathlons, he understands the great confidence athletic achievement can instill.

Just like David and his team, those of us who are active in Achilles borrow from our own personal experiences – leading organizations, participating in marathons, encouraging and mentoring those with physical and emotional disabilities and inviting others to join us.

We've watched individuals literally pick themselves up and demonstrate incredible courage and determination. Today, they are 5K finishers. They are marathon finishers. They are Ironman finishers. They are inspiring others to push themselves, get to the start line and go the distance. What excites us most is that anything is possible, and we've seen how – with the right support system and encouragement – individuals can make their goals a reality. They can exceed anything they could have accomplished on their own.

The partnership between Cigna and Achilles, which began in 2008 and has progressively grown in many wonderful ways, is a powerful example of how creating micro communities can motivate others to go beyond what they ever thought was possible.

In our case, we're combining our resources to help people with many kinds of disabilities to view themselves as athletes. That's our passion; yours could be one of hundreds of others, from working with underprivileged children or raising awareness of vital social issues to motivating friends and colleagues to take on a significant societal challenge.

The success and the passion of our employees, members and volunteers remind us there has never been a greater need for active and passionate micro communities than there is today.

David Cordani and Dick Traum

A Path Emerges

2018 Boston Marathon

From David: How Our Partnership Began

In 2012, when I arrived at Disney for the Walt Disney World® Marathon Weekend, Cigna had already been supporting individuals with disabilities, illnesses and injuries through our long-term disability insurance program. Cigna and the Cigna Foundation had also been providing financial support to Achilles International, and many of our employees were involved in Achilles events, serving as volunteers and guides for disabled runners.

My personal involvement began when I attended my first Achilles event months before the Walt Disney World Marathon and immediately saw a family working together to bring hope, inspiration and support to those with special needs. I was so impressed and thought Achilles did amazing work. I had to get involved.

When I approached Achilles team members and asked for the opportunity to guide one of the team's runners through a race, they immediately put me in contact with a member of Achilles's Freedom Team, the organization's wounded veterans program. He and I completed the 2012 Walt Disney World Half Marathon together, and it was a highly emotional moment for me. Watching people from all walks of life helping each other, making sure they had everything they needed to get to the starting line and complete the 13-mile course was overwhelming.

After the Disney event, I thought about how much more these two organizations could accomplish – there was so much that the collective "we" could do. The Cigna/Achilles community had embraced the power of possibility and planted the seeds that, ultimately, would grow into a motivated, valuable community. But our partnership in its early days was not used to its full potential, so we needed to determine which seeds to fertilize and cultivate. We had more to achieve.

It was time to aggressively build on our power of partnership.

Participant at
Walt Disney
World® Marathon
Weekend presented
by Cigna
©Disney

From Dick: A Partnership Rooted in Passion

The night before the 2012 Walt Disney World Half Marathon, David hosted a reception for employees and friends of Achilles as part of his partnership with us, and I was struck by his energy. Wearing an Achilles T-shirt, he welcomed everyone and gave us a memorable pep talk that rippled with a tangible spirit of inclusion and optimism. It was difficult not to be inspired by his amazing level of commitment and purpose. Not surprisingly, this man could work a room.

At the reception, David and I mingled, having our pictures taken and encouraging everyone to have a great event. I noticed neither one of us had a desire to take over and control the room. We avoided being the center of attention and focused more on our people, and on nurturing this family dynamic we had created together.

Watching David more closely, I had to laugh because he was clearly using the same social skills and techniques as me, but at a much higher level. I figured I must have been doing the right thing.

Another interesting thing was that David shared my dyed-in-the-wool, bleeding-heart optimism, and for this we made no apologies. We both took great pleasure in inspiring and motivating others, and we understood the importance of demonstrating integrity, commitment and optimism.

The following day during the half marathon, I had the honor of accompanying a man named Tyler Southern and one of his friends from Walter Reed National Military Medical Center. Like so many Achilles athletes, Tyler has a remarkable story. On his second deployment to Afghanistan in 2010, Tyler had stepped on an improvised explosive device (IED). As a result, he lost both legs above the knee and his right arm above the elbow. Yet here he was, competing in his first race. I realized

Participant at Walt Disney World® Marathon Weekend presented by Cigna
©Disney

early on that Tyler shared my unusual sense of humor when he showed up wearing a T-shirt emblazoned with "Had a blast in Afghanistan" across the chest. Priceless.

At first, we moved along at a nine-minute pace, and all was fine. But somewhere after the seven-mile mark, as we cruised down a steep hill and started to climb the next knoll, Tyler's handcycle turned over. I asked how he was feeling and noticed he was clearly winded. We took a timeout. A few minutes later, I helped him back into the handcycle, and he comfortably finished the race in a little under two hours.

Tyler was beaming. It was one of the greatest days of his life. And when he returned to Walter Reed, people saw him differently. His success at Disney inspired him to immediately redefine his sense of self and identify new goals. He was a hero not only to himself, but also to everyone who knew him. His spirit was contagious!

As we spoke about the event, Tyler said something surprising. Instead of describing me as being helpful and caring like a father, he said I was supportive and like a grandfather! I had progressed one generation in Tyler's mind, while his progress over the Disney course was immeasurable. That was a fair trade-off, I suppose.

The more I thought about it, David and I had become elder statesmen, too. We certainly had similar business trajectories – from motivating small staffs to becoming supervisors and then progressing beyond to manage supervisors.

It was also like this in our personal lives, where we progressed from being the youngster who runs and competes, to the adult who supervises and manages other runners, and then progressing beyond that to become the elder statesman, making sure our people have everything they need to help others succeed.

It became clear to me that David also received tremendous joy from helping others achieve. I thought about the impact we made, getting athletes out there on the course who most likely would never have done so on their own had we not started Achilles. Like Tyler, many people with disabilities consider a day like this as one of the greatest days, if not the greatest day, in their lives. And that makes us ecstatic.

Following the 2012 Walt Disney World Half Marathon, Cigna and Achilles continued to develop a game plan. Cigna had disabled clients and Achilles was relentlessly looking for new members. What a match: Cigna and Achilles!

Achilles increased its membership and Cigna helped its disabled clients become physically fit. Inspiring people to expand their horizons, set goals and be successful is a philosophy shared by both organizations.

With our shared goals and passion in mind, we imagined the power of our for-profit/nonprofit partnership and the possibilities of what we could achieve together.

A grateful Tri-Achilles Team
at Lido Beach Triathlon

THE COURAGE TO GO FORWARD

02

THE POWER OF POSSIBILITIES

"The world is more malleable than you think and it's waiting for you to hammer it into shape."

– Bono

From David: The Golden Rule

In 2015, I served as an Achilles guide during the Boston Marathon and helped an Achilles runner come face to face with his willpower, determination and resolve. Our journey reinforced a fundamental principle we can all embrace throughout our lives: The Golden Rule.

We'd been slogging through mile seven of the 2015 Boston Marathon for what seemed like ages, the veteran and I, under a torrent of cold, wind and rain. The trifecta. Take just one of the three and it's dismal. Try handling all three for 26.2 miles and it is beyond miserable.

My partner makes his way using prosthetics, having lost both legs serving as an Army Ranger in Afghanistan in 2012. Here, some 19 miles from the finish line, a handful of drenched spectators cheer us on as I try to remember other equally horrible weather conditions in my two dozen years of racing. Very few, if any, come to mind. On this day, we just wanted to finish.

But while I grimaced about the weather, I knew my comrade, Master Sergeant Cedric King, had suffered much worse. He was on his second tour in Afghanistan when an IED explosion tore through him, causing major internal injuries, permanent loss to part of his right arm and hand and the amputation of both legs.

Recuperating at Walter Reed National Military Medical Center, Cedric was not nearly as alone or downcast as he thought he would be. That's because several people from Achilles were on the scene, many of them amputees and wounded warriors themselves, offering words of encouragement and an invitation to get up, move on and join them on the road to recovery.

With their inspiration – along with the love and support of his wife, Khieda, and daughters, Amari and Khayma – he learned to walk on prosthetic legs. "At first," King says, "after just 10 minutes walking on prosthetics, I was exhausted. I scoffed and told them I could never run a marathon. They said, 'Yes, you can.'" He began to engage in his recovery with the same steadfast tenacity that marked his success as an elite Army Ranger.

Before too long, I was paired with him as an Achilles running guide, and we established a good, trusting rapport through several

David Cordani and Cedric King
at the 2015 Boston Marathon

races. "I quickly realized the important role David played and I knew I wanted him in my foxhole," Cedric would say.

Our strong bond was about to be tested that day in Boston.

With the rain pelting us as though we were running through a 26-mile car wash, with 19 miles to go, Cedric and I were about to have a trifecta of our own: a flood of anger, frustration and profanity.

Although we had been through some tough times in the past, this was going to be brutal. We were on the ground, which happens during races sometimes. His prosthetics were off, and we were doing our best to dry the stumps in the driving rain. This would be the first of many moments over the course of the day when Cedric wanted to abandon the race. He sat on the ground as I tried to put his prosthetics back on. Things were getting testy.

"What in the world are you doing?!" I looked up and two FBI-like guys were hovering over me, shouting as I wrestled with Cedric. It looked like I was beating the hell out of this guy – a rain-drenched, double amputee. I took a deep breath, looked up and said to the SWAT team, "I got this!" No hesitation, no push back, no sign of retaliation, just two guys realizing what's going on. They gave way.

Cedric stared at me with steely eyes and said, "I'm going to kick your ass." I knew him well enough to see the way to his soul. This man was a warrior, and it was time to challenge his core identity.

"Your call," I said, "but if you tap out, it's all on you."

Again, he promised, "I'm going to kick your ass."

"So why don't you save that energy for the finish line?" I responded. "Then, we can throw down." He resisted a bit more until he let me put his prosthetics back on. We got him up, looked at each other and started back. We had many miles to go.

Multiple times that day he squinted at me and repeated, "I'm going to kick your ass at the finish line." Seven wretched hours later, we crossed the finish line, dog-tired yet feeling as if we had just completed a great chapter in our lives. I immediately put him into a wheelchair, Cedric reminded me one last time that he was the toughest sergeant in the U.S. Army, saying "I still have to kick your ass."

"You want to do that now or later?"

"I'll do that later," he said with a grin.

After drying up and getting some more liquids in us, we got into the car to head out, basking in a mutual glow of success and assurance, having gone through a collective fire and emerging triumphant on the other side. "I need to ask you one question," he said. "Did you hurt out there at all?"

"Why are you asking?" I asked.

"You showed no pain, no frustration, no discomfort at any point in time," he said. "Did you hurt at all?"

I felt my aching back. "I hurt in ways that you can't imagine," I told him honestly.

"Why didn't you show it?" he asked.

I told him that wasn't my role. "If I showed it, it would have been easier for you to feel pain, too. So, I boxed it."

> "Oh, dear God, thank you," he said, happily. "I thought you were a f***ing android!"

Now, Cedric and I have an ongoing connection, deep shared experiences and some unfinished business. At some point he still has to kick my ass!

PROFILES IN COURAGE

David Cordani and Cedric King
at Walt Disney World® Marathon
Weekend presented by Cigna
©Disney

THE COURAGE TO GO FORWARD

Cedric King

Ret. Master Sergeant, U.S. Army | Georgia

The day before the 2015 Boston Marathon, I was with David at a Red Sox game, and the weather was beautiful – 65 degrees and a nice Boston day. I said, "Man, if the weather's like this tomorrow, we're going to have a ball." Overnight, the temperature dropped into the 30s and at race time, it was starting to sleet. It was just the worst possible conditions.

To David's credit, it was still the fastest I had ever run a marathon – seven hours. It was even better than my time at Disney, where we run in perfect conditions. But that year in Boston, under the worst circumstances, I performed my best.

David is the guy you want in the foxhole beside you. Because he'll give you everything he's got, and he won't complain. That's one of the things I noticed during the Boston run. I did not hear this man complain one time about his own discomfort. He was always saying, "Hey Cedric, let's go. Let's go. Let's pick it up. Let's go."

David Cordani and Cedric King at Walt Disney
World® Marathon Weekend presented by Cigna
©Disney

He never allowed me to feel sorry for myself, either. He didn't look at me as a handicapped dude. He didn't look at me as someone without legs. He looked at me as another competitor on the race course. And that's very rare.

At the end of the race, I needed to know if he was putting it all out there. He could have easily run faster. But I also know that it's easier to run a four-hour marathon than a seven-hour marathon, and that's why I asked him whether he was tired. It's hard to run a bit slower if you don't have a pair of legs missing. It's easier to push yourself to speed up rather than to slow down. For me, I knew that he had given it all. But I needed to hear it from him at the time.

I remember when I was at Walter Reed and the people from Achilles were the only outside people I had met in that entire first year and a half. They said, "We believe in you. Go get it and we'll back you."

It wasn't, "Oh, well, we don't know if you'll get hurt or not." It was, "Here's your bib number. Here's your T-shirt. Let's get to the start line. Let's go." Every single run and nearly everything I've done athletically, Achilles helped me get to the start line.

> When I got injured, I didn't just lose my legs – I lost part of my identity, too.

While I was at Walter Reed, Achilles reintroduced me to the Cedric that I knew before – to the competitor, the fighter, the soldier and the Ranger. When you have lost your identity, you need people to reintroduce you to who you used to be, and that reintroduction showed me who I could be.

Achilles gave me the push I needed. The community said, "We don't know if you can do it and you don't know if you can do it. But let's find out." Everybody needs somebody who says, "Let's get in the ring, put the gloves on and find out what you've got."

The key is to give yourself a chance and put the right people around you who are willing to go the distance with you.

The Journey Awaits

2018 Boston Marathon

From David: Failure is Not an Option

My experience with Cedric during the 2015 Boston Marathon reminds me of the power every one of us has within ourselves to pursue seemingly impossible goals, overcome enormous obstacles, persevere and reach the finish line.

He could have quit. He could have given up. He could have kicked my ass and abandoned me on the course. But for him – and for me as his guide and advocate – failure was not an option.

"Failure is not an option" can be the mindset of a small, impassioned group of one, two or three of us to live by. This is the power of "yes, I can do this!"

There is a fundamental life principle based on the concept of "when you give to others, you also benefit." While Dick and I have different backgrounds, and we first met as adults, we were not raised dissimilarly from one another. Both our parents and grandparents inspired us to be what we call givers – in other words, we were raised to follow the Golden Rule – to treat others as we hope they would treat us.

We were raised to make a difference in people's lives, and to give our time, energy and commitment to do it. As it relates to this idea of micro communities, givers are typically individuals who genuinely want to help and support someone, share with others and find true joy in the process. Givers also believe that anything is possible. They have an inborn capacity to persevere through every obstacle, maintain their focus and achieve seemingly impossible things.

The fact is, no matter how successful anyone becomes, few achieve their goals by themselves. All of us need others to help us on our life journeys. That's where givers come in. They share their skills, time, knowledge and experience to help others more easily close the gap between their aspirations and actual achievements.

With givers at our side, we – and by "we," I mean everyone – can persevere and find the "finish line."

Micro Communities

Dick and I have come to appreciate the force of smaller, tight-knit groups of two, three or more people coming together for a finite period of time, with a high level of selflessness and oriented around a goal shared between us. A small group of like-minded people can empower an individual to overcome obstacles and achieve his or her goals in a life-changing way. Specifically, the group dynamic can empower individuals to confront their perceived personal limitations, set audacious goals, overcome their fears and achieve beyond their wildest expectations – to forge a path they may not have pursued alone.

This common experience, driven by a specific purpose or goal and formed through myriad activities, is what we call a micro community. Regardless of the end result – be it running a race, acquiring a skill or simply becoming a healthier person – the potential impact is enormous.

A micro community is a means by which individuals, such as the disabled veterans who participate in Achilles events, can pursue their goals with the benefit of endless love and encouragement. It is a place where they can be themselves and aspire to achieve something great.

For Dick and me, being a part of a micro community means our sense of self becomes rooted in proven beliefs and established principles. As we search to understand our own place in the world, we often harken back to the family units where our core values and principles took shape.

Again, for Dick and me, personal attachment to others begins when we participate together, whether in community events, social functions or political organizations. "We cannot live only for ourselves," Herman Melville, author of Moby Dick, wrote. "A thousand fibers connect us with our fellow men."

When we begin to see the potential in every individual, the spirit in every person and the passion in everyone, we then realize the potential of a well-intentioned micro community.

Uniting to focus on achievement is the greatest undertaking we can accomplish. "One of the marvelous things about community is that it enables us to welcome and help people in a way we couldn't as individuals," wrote the Canadian philosopher, theologian and humanitarian Jean Vanier. A micro community is rooted in the spirit of a close-knit family, buoyed by their energy, determination and passion for advancing every member.

Often, micro communities begin with just a few givers and a clear mission, but then attract others who are equally impassioned and motivated. Support and resources from sponsors and partners help to grow the network, expand the reach and broaden its influence. Whether it's through social services organizations or larger social media networks, we see individuals moving toward micro communities that deliver more meaningful, personalized and real-time engagement.

As we look more closely, we see the formation of both situational and sustainable micro communities that, far more often than not, benefit everyone involved – the givers as well as those they help.

Elzbieta Gorgon, first female double amputee to run the New York City Marathon

Situational Micro Communities

In August 2017, when Hurricane Harvey tore through Houston, I remember a photo, published in a local newspaper: About 25 people from every walk of life, complete strangers, had formed a human chain to navigate chest-high water and rescue an elderly man trapped in an SUV. They were the embodiment of a situational micro community – humanity borne out of a crisis – giving of themselves in a momentary point in time. Their positive attitude inspired action. Their collective reinforcement, camaraderie and a shared experience came into play, as well.

Dick and I see this kind of selfless attitude every day: people coming from different walks of life but with a shared experience. It could be working together during a natural disaster. It could be helping someone on a 5K run. It could be a marathon. It could be a handcycle race. It could be working with an autistic child. No matter what the challenge is, people are inspired by their collective spirit to get off the couch and get involved. That's the power of possibility: Set a goal, overcome obstacles and achieve something that's pretty damned cool.

Events such as the Hurricane Harvey recovery demonstrate how micro communities are motivated to achieve wonderfully heroic things when a crisis calls. Someone jumps into a burning car and saves those who are trapped inside. Two people come together to hoist someone out of a collapsed building.

But they are usually motivated by a momentary crisis that triggers an instinctive reaction. The question is: How can we, as a society, develop more micro communities when there's not a crisis? Can there be a more deliberate, proactive and positive intent to achieve something special?

Melissa Wilcox's determination to create Philly Achilles is an example of a situational micro community – not one established during a time of crisis, but as a proactive measure – built around the energy and sheer fortitude of a single person to make a profound change.

After serving as a guide to a visually impaired athlete during the 2012 Walt Disney World Half Marathon, Melissa was hooked on Achilles. When she returned home and learned there was no Achilles chapter in her hometown of Philadelphia, she was determined to pull a team together to establish one. In true Achilles fashion, she believed failure was not an option.

Today, Philly Achilles has become the model for a micro community, transforming from the profound courage of one person with a vision into a community with a diverse range of disabled athletes and more than a hundred dedicated volunteers, inspiring several new micro communities within it.

Philly Achilles continues to define the value of a micro community, expanding and leveraging the power of possibilities. Whether formed during a moment of crisis or created to carry out a very deliberate undertaking, all micro communities need just two simple qualities: a shared purpose and a shared goal.

Like those created during Hurricane Harvey, situational micro communities can be short-lived and have a specific purpose for a finite period of time. But many times, they unfold and transform. As Melissa Wilcox puts it, the "encouragement, support, friendship and inspiration to be experienced is bountiful."

PROFILES IN COURAGE

Melissa Wilcox running with
Achilles athlete Kinzey Lynch

Melissa Wilcox

HR Operations Project Manager, Cigna
President, Philadelphia Chapter, Achilles | Pennsylvania

It was a bit daunting at first, but I decided that if I wanted an Achilles chapter in Philadelphia, I needed to take action to start it myself. Our Cigna Civic Affairs group gave me a grant to help start the chapter because there were costs involved in getting insurance, our shirts and everything we needed to start up. I quickly recruited some of my Cigna friends and my running friends to help with the chapter and also to run with us because I wanted to make sure we had at least a handful of people our first day. For our very first workout, we had three athletes come – one was in a wheelchair, one was visually impaired and the third one had recently been in a car accident and just needed some rehab walking to get back into the swing of things.

From there, our core team continued the legwork, going to various groups within the community to recruit volunteers and find athletes. In the first couple of months, through word of mouth, we recruited several more visually impaired runners and people with autism, amputees and people who had handcycles. We very quickly expanded and were fortunate that all of the athletes immediately fell in love with the whole experience. Even though many of them lived pretty far away – some over an hour by train or by car – they loyally traveled to come to our workouts every Saturday.

Cigna was kind enough to let us use the employee fitness center in Philly on Saturdays. So, we actually have a place to meet, which makes it very convenient for people to come and have a place to keep their stuff.

We've been around for five-and-a-half years, and we have a very close-knit chapter. Our Facebook group is called the "Philly Achilles Family," which is what we're all about. When we come and we meet up, we don't just head straight out for a run or a walk. A lot of people call us a social club instead of a running club because sometimes we talk and talk and procrastinate. We meet at 9 a.m. and sometimes don't get moving until 9:20 a.m., but it makes the experience more fun.

> One of my favorite parts of every workout is when I first walk in and Andrew Kessler gives me a big hug.

He's autistic, and between the train ride, the run and the socialization, Saturday mornings have become his favorite time of the week! For most, it really is like a second family. And we have a lot of parties afterward because we have a place that has become our designated post-run meeting spot. It's awesome.

When I show up for our Saturday morning workouts and I see the people there all laughing and chatting, and really just inspiring each other and changing lives, it's humbling. We have amazing people that helped get this off the ground. I could not have done it without them.

Melissa Wilcox running with
Achilles athlete Kinzey Lynch

Sustainable Micro Communities

Sometimes, a small, situational micro community can evolve into a longer-term sustainable micro community, coming together for extended and ongoing periods of time with a clear goal and a larger group of highly motivated members.

A good example of a situational micro community that transformed into a more sustainable enterprise involved Trisha Meili – better known to the public as the "Central Park Jogger."

In the summer of 1989, Trisha was rehabilitating at the Gaylord Hospital based in Wallingford, Conn., after she was attacked, beaten and raped in Central Park in New York. She was left with a traumatic brain injury, which led to severe physical and cognitive dysfunction. Gaylord's director of physical therapy suggested that she join Achilles' Gaylord Connecticut Chapter, a group that spent weekends running together. A woman who could barely walk just weeks earlier, Trisha started running with the Gaylord members.

At first, Trisha recalled being barely able to walk around the quarter-mile loop through the hospital's parking lot. She worked hard and bonded with her fellow Gaylord members. By the time she left the Gaylord facility, Trisha was jogging four miles – an incredible example of bringing the power of possibilities to life.

"By the time she left the Gaylord facility, Trisha was jogging four miles – an incredible example of bringing the power of possibilities to life."

PROFILES IN COURAGE

Dick Traum and Trisha Meili

Trisha Meili

Best-selling author, *I Am the Central Park Jogger:
A Story of Hope and Possibility*

I so clearly remember that first run around the quarter-mile loop and how I wasn't sure if I could make it. But I had this group of people around me, and there was a sense of not going alone. I was unsteady for a lot of it, but when we approached the "finish line," it just felt so good and I wondered whether I could do another loop around. I felt like I could conquer the world, and it filled me with such hope!

I felt it in my soul and thought, "Wow. Look at what I'm doing. What else might be possible?"

> The deep feeling of connection with this group of people gave me such joy because I could share my achievement with them.

It was a sign of appreciating where I was and enjoying the moment, being realistic, realizing this was good and that there would be time to build on it. I was taking something back that had been taken away.

Dick Traum and
Trisha Meili

Trisha Meili joining the post-
race celebration at the Hope &
Possibility® Race.

Even in those early days at Gaylord, I started to focus on what I could do, rather than on my deficits. A sense of hope was building because of my therapists and all of the support I was getting. I was fortunate to have this wonderful support system around me that was so important to my recovery. Through the aerobic activity, I kept moving– getting better and stronger – and this seemed to have a positive effect on my cognitive rehabilitation. On the physical side, we set small goals and gradually increased them. Seeing my physical and cognitive improvement made me feel better about myself and gave me the confidence to push harder.

I believe deep within each of us, we have a resource to heal or come to terms with whatever is our challenge.

> Through the love and support of others, we gain a sense of hope, unleashing the willpower to move forward and do more.

This is exactly what Achilles does.

It gives each of us a sense of hope and from that, possibility emerges, whether it's the possibility of completing a quarter-mile loop or running a marathon. I admire Dick for having this vision – and perhaps it became more than he ever imagined. Everyone feels it, and it just keeps growing – this whole community that comes together for each other.

Within Achilles, everyone ends up giving and receiving without really knowing it. We often hear from able-bodied guides that they get more out of the experience than the person they are guiding. The guides feel an incredible attachment to the athletes and to that sense of achievement and confidence-building, which bolsters them. Everyone benefits – givers and receivers, which really is the beauty and magic of Achilles.

When we held the first Hope & Possibility® Race in Central Park in 2003, we had no more than 200 people. It was a fabulous day, and now the race sells out every year! I'm always at the finish line, because I just love encouraging people, and I get strength from watching and being a part of their special day.

From my spot on the finish line, watching these athletes achieve their goals is so powerful that I can just tell – from the looks on the spectators' faces – they are thinking, "If they can do that, I can do whatever I want, too." This is one of the gifts that those with challenges provide.

From Dick: Hope and Possibility

I remember running the 1994 New York City Marathon with Trisha, and our early start placed us nine miles ahead of the leading runners. When we finished the marathon, Trisha said, "This isn't too hard. I think I'll run it myself next year." Being on the course that day inspired Trisha to achieve something she never thought she could. She formed a small Achilles group and set a goal, completing the 1995 New York City Marathon in 4:30, faster than the average finisher. A situational micro community was born.

Trisha discussed her profound cognitive improvement with Dr. Wayne Gordon, a professor of rehabilitation medicine at the Icahn School of Medicine at Mount Sinai in New York. Dr. Gordon was conducting a study on exercise and cognition, and he invited her to be one of the co-authors on what would become the first study concerning cognitive improvement associated with exercise and running.

Because of her passion, Trisha earned attention at the national level of the Achilles organization. We invited Trisha to join our board of directors, and she eventually became our first board chair. To this day, she is our most active board member.

When Trisha decided to tell her story in The New York Times best seller I Am the Central Park Jogger: A Story of Hope and Possibility, we had moved our annual Achilles Marathon race from Brooklyn to a five-miler in Central Park. Why not name the race after her book to help inspire others?

Trisha's energy and commitment to Achilles inspired us to establish the annual Hope & Possibility Race through Central Park, which debuted on June 29, 2003, and now attracts several thousand participants every year. Awards are presented specifically for athletes with disabilities in various categories, including Pushrim Wheelchair, Handcycle, Power Chair, Ambulatory Disabled, Above and Below Knee Amputee, Double Amputee and Visually Impaired.

Thus, a sustainable micro community had been borne out of the smaller group of runners Trisha had joined some eight years earlier.

2018 Boston Marathon

2018 Boston Marathon

THE COURAGE TO GO FORWARD

03

COMMUNITIES IN ACTION

"If your actions inspire others to dream more, learn more, do more and become more, you are a leader."

— John Quincy Adams

Lessons from David and Dick

We believe that whether it's someone with a physical disability such as Cedric King, someone with a cognitive disability such as Trisha Meili, someone confronting a medical challenge or one who simply sets a personal goal, each of us has a unique life and health journey.

Each of us also has the capacity to establish goals and objectives – in many cases seemingly unattainable or perhaps only aspirational in nature – and harness the willpower to achieve them.

Willpower – our drive and determination – can only take us so far. We also recognize the importance of creating and following a prearranged recipe – a path or road map for how we can visualize our journey and actually reach our goals.

Kat Bateman leading a New York City Chapter workout

2018 Boston Marathon

The Recipe

A good recipe is one of the keys to harnessing the power of a micro community. Like anything we prepare in the kitchen, the final product is only as good as the quality of the ingredients we assemble.

2018 Boston Marathon

Here is a basic six-step recipe to help us achieve our most ambitious goals:

1. **Define the Vision:** The process for setting clear objectives and taking the steps to achieve them begins with establishing the vision: a true north point of direction that guides everyone on the journey.

2. **Create a Strategy:** Having a clear strategy defines how we are going to achieve our vision. Built into the strategy is a plan of action – the hard work and sense of purpose to get there.

3. **Attract the Right Resources:** We rely on our people, research and development teams, and other resources to help us build an infrastructure to get programs off the ground and sustain them over the long term.

4. **Execute to Achieve the Plan:** Once we define our aspirations and create a strategy, the ultimate difference between success and failure is our ability to execute and achieve the plan.

5. **Overcome Obstacles:** No matter how foolproof our recipe may be, we should always anticipate obstacles, setbacks and a few stumbles along the way. Be prepared to adjust accordingly.

6. **Expand and Grow:** Just as recipes evolve when they are passed down through generations or modified with healthier ingredients, our basic recipe allows us to make improvements and expand the vision with new opportunities across more micro communities.

The ingredients of our recipe are best conveyed through stories about our employees, volunteers and members – the individuals who define, promote and advance the tenets of our micro community. We have come to appreciate the value of sharing short accounts that inspire us, provide meaning to our experiences and give us a sense of belonging.

In addition to Cedric King's, Melissa Wilcox's and Trisha Meili's Profiles in Courage in the previous chapter, we also have also included several more throughout these pages to highlight the athletes and their own perspectives on how they've overcome challenges and achieved great things with the help of others.

01 | Define the Vision

The process for setting clear objectives and taking the steps to achieve them begins with establishing the vision: a true north point of direction that guides everyone on the journey.

From David: Know What You Want to Achieve

Let me share an example of establishing a vision based on a project I've been involved with.

While recent reports show encouraging signs that obesity rates are stabilizing, and even declining in certain populations in the United States, rates still remain too high in all age groups. Furthermore, disparities exist along racial, ethnic, socio-economic and geographic lines. While obesity rates may decline overall, these inequities will persist unless intentional action is taken.

The causes of obesity are complex and interconnected; culture, societal norms and practices at home all influence a child's ability to make healthy choices and influence weight status.

The micro community of talented leaders we brought together from across academia, business, government and the nonprofit world for the ChildObesity180 initiative had a clear vision: to develop, measure and apply evidence-based solutions to reverse the alarming epidemic of childhood obesity in America.

Based at the Friedman School of Nutrition Science and Policy at Tufts University, this micro community of experts came together to:

- Work on school breakfast improvement, delivery, administration and advocacy.

- Study the effect on obesity of providing a program called "Breakfast in the Classroom" in a large, urban school district.

- Share the study results and other critical information with researchers, school administrators, advocates and partners.

We set out to reach school-aged children who were disproportionately affected by obesity, defining our vision and following a recipe for schools, communities and other organizations to create their own micro communities to address this important issue.

At the time, we had just read Chip and Dan Heath's book, Switch: How to Change Things When Change Is Hard. We learned about how we can define successes worth emulating – called "bright spots" – to help articulate a vision and script our critical moves. Instead of asking, "What's broken, and how do we fix it?", we must focus on the "bright spots" and instead ask, "What is working, and how can we do more of it?"

Bright spots always exist if you look hard enough. With this in mind, we asked teachers, administrators and parents for their input and generated thousands of suggestions that became the foundation of our program.

Among our many ChildObesity180 programs, we launched the Active Schools Acceleration Project (ASAP) – a major initiative, endorsed by then-First Lady, Michelle Obama, to promote more physical activity at schools. Today, nearly 10,000 schools participate in ASAP programs.

For these ChildObesity180 initiatives, the team focused on building a technological solution to assimilate the myriad ideas we generated. Once the vision was established, we asked for the team's insights, and this became the impetus for creating our recipe for success. The next step was to apply our strategy school by school so they, in turn, could create micro communities based on our common goals.

———

As we begin to formulate our recipe, there's no question that before we can act, we need to articulate the vision. Within a micro community, the leader communicates the vision to like-minded individuals and inspires them to think of new ways to help and contribute. Leaders move people to act on the vision, which defines the underlying spirit of the micro community because it ultimately forces us to answer the question, "What do we want to achieve?"

More often, the vision begins when leaders articulate the expectations and the mission of the team. Leaders are role models; they set the example and drive sustainability within the micro community. When others see the potential of the vision, they want to follow suit and do it on their own, in turn, creating more new micro communities.

The vision for ChildObesity180 was about integrating the mission of a nonprofit organization into the culture of a for-profit corporation, and we knew it was time to roll up our sleeves and get to work. Our goal was to motivate people to act, either by giving their time and support or by setting a goal to achieve and being open to getting results.

This also became the driving force behind the Cigna/Achilles partnership, and I began recognizing just how profoundly my experience with Achilles was shaping my worldview. I now saw a whole world of possibility about how for-profit and nonprofit organizations could partner to create enormous opportunities for our employees, volunteers and members.

My experience as a running guide inspired me to push both Cigna and Achilles to grow our partnership and find new ways to make a greater impact on people with disabilities. Today, our Cigna/Achilles micro community has a shared vision to train and inspire disabled individuals to participate in running events, so they can continue on their journey to health, productivity and achievement. We work hand in hand to help individuals achieve more than they ever thought they could and inspire them to motivate others as autonomous, yet interdependent, extensions of our micro community.

―――――

We see time and again that having a sense of purpose and direction, and knowing your "true north" – what's really important to you – can mean everything.

Kathy Strickland admits that even after she was diagnosed with cancer, she didn't really know how to react because she just didn't feel all that different. Then she started treatment and the side effects and frequent doctor appointments really began to impact her life. In fact, she had to stop working, which for her was among the most devastating effects of all.

Luckily for Kathy, a Cigna vocational coach understood the situation and had a suggestion that could possibly hasten Kathy's return to work – a walking program to help rebuild Kathy's physical endurance.

Kathy agreed.

At first, Kathy could walk the length of only seven houses without tiring. But she persevered, day by day, house by house.

Soon, it was 22 houses, then 78. It didn't actually seem all that far to Kathy until one day she drove the length of those 78 houses and saw that she'd actually been walking more than two miles.

And then her vocational coach told Kathy about an upcoming 5K walking event.

Kathy welcomed the idea of having a program to build her stamina, to build her strength and to ultimately return to work. It gave her hope, and helped her to keep believing when she didn't know what the future held for her.

Perhaps Kathy's most satisfying was getting back to work. Once again, the vision was defined and a micro community established – something that everyone involved was truly proud to be part of.

PROFILES IN COURAGE

THE COURAGE TO GO FORWARD

Kathy Strickland

Cigna Collaborative Care Customer | Texas

I didn't even know what a 5K was. But I immediately said yes. Support is very important, and...I appreciated that about (Cigna).

Hope is for your future...to be able to be here to see my grandchildren go to school, get their diplomas, even to graduate from college – to see them get married.

To know that I'm here for them when they need me.

02 | Create a Strategy

Having a clear strategy defines how we are going to achieve our vision. Built into the strategy is a plan of action – the hard work and sense of purpose to get there.

From Dick: The Path from Hospital Bed to Marathon Course

When I arrived in the Motor City for the start of the 2016 Detroit Marathon, I surveyed the sea of participants and thought about how time had flown by. At 75, I was one of the oldest competitors.

Forty years had passed since I ran the 1976 New York City Marathon on an artificial leg. I thought back to the moment I crossed my first marathon finish line, having put 26.2 miles behind me one difficult stride at a time. There was media attention from the New York Daily News and Runner's World.

My training and hard work had paid off and I had a renewed sense of purpose, which motivated me from that point forward. After 1976, people saw me in a different light and their positive impression of me was a powerful incentive. I was no longer a disabled individual with a weakness. I was a marathoner. I wondered whether I could motivate others with disabilities to realize that more was possible.

Some years later, Achilles International would introduce people with disabilities to long-distance running. Our members represented disability groups that included the visually impaired, amputees, people with multiple sclerosis, paraplegics, people who had suffered traumatic brain injuries, people with diabetes and people with learning disabilities, autism and cerebral palsy – and they were realizing they could do almost anything if they just took the first step (literally and figuratively).

In 2016 in Detroit, 29 of our Achilles Freedom Team members waited at the start line. Injured in tours in Iraq and Afghanistan, each had lost as many as three limbs. Many also suffered from mental health issues, including post-traumatic stress disorder (PTSD). The Freedom Team participated in physical conditioning and confidence building, and had a supportive community behind them. These veterans worked with motivated physical therapists to address their needs.

Two members of our Freedom Team competing in Detroit were Alfredo De Los Santos and Tom Davis. Alfredo encountered a rocket-propelled grenade while serving in Afghanistan. He is a right-leg amputee and suffered from a traumatic brain injury, hearing loss and PTSD. Tom's left leg was amputated above the knee when a roadside bomb destroyed his Humvee while he was serving in Iraq.

Thanks to training and hard work, Alfredo and Tom were regarded as the best competitors in the world. Alfredo and Tom represented Team USA in the 2016 Paralympics and finished just seconds behind the winner at the Rio 2016 Paralympic Games. In Detroit, they held hands and cranked their handcycles across the finish line in 1:08:39, breaking the course record by six minutes.

Freedom Team members like Alfredo and Tom remind me of the rags-to-riches Horatio Alger stories kids from my generation grew up reading. These young warriors had gone from a bed in an intensive care unit of a military hospital to completing a marathon. They took a hit in war, survived and returned to life by achieving and mainstreaming. Their spirit of achievement is woven into our Achilles mission: to enable people with all types of physical and mental challenges to participate in mainstream athletics and to promote personal achievement.

One of the most memorable stories I heard was about a soldier who wanted so badly to participate in a marathon, but needed yet another surgery to repair his wounds. He pleaded with his surgeon, "Sir, may I postpone my surgery to next week so I can compete in a marathon on Sunday?"

That's the spirit!

PROFILES IN COURAGE

THE COURAGE TO GO FORWARD

Alfredo De Los Santos

Ret. Staff Sergeant, U.S. Army | New York

On Oct. 20, 2008, while serving in the area southwest of Forward Operating Base Price in Central Helmand Providence, Afghanistan, I was wounded in action when my vehicle received fire from a rocket-propelled grenade. As a consequence of the blast, I lost my right leg above the knee, received dental trauma and have hearing loss, PTSD and Traumatic Brain Injury.

For two years, I had to work extremely hard to gain independency and transition to a normal life. It was not an easy road, but I was determined to push myself.

> At the hospital all the support I received was overwhelming, but it wasn't until I met the members of Achilles that my life began to turn around.

I still remember when they asked me if I was interested in doing a marathon. My initial reaction was, "There's no way I can do a marathon." At the time I was very weak, in really bad shape and I could hardly stand up. I was not mentally recuperated enough to even leave my room. But I accepted their challenge and competed my first-ever marathon with the support of Achilles.

Yes, I did it!

Through my participation as a wounded vet in the Achilles program, I started to gain strength, endurance and self-confidence while I improved my quality of life. Achilles has greatly helped me recover not just physically, but also socially and mentally. Being able to compete in marathons, despite my disability, has been the most rewarding experience of my life. Through my participation as an Achilles athlete, I try to bring hope, inspiration and the joy of achievement to people with disabilities. I decided to become an elite athlete to prove to myself that I can't stand up, but now – thanks to Achilles – I stand out.

PROFILES IN COURAGE

Alfredo De Los Santos
at 2018 Boston Marathon

PROFILES IN COURAGE

THE COURAGE TO GO FORWARD

Tom Davis

Ret. Staff Sergeant, U.S. Army | Indiana

My physical therapist at Walter Reed knew I was an athlete, so one day he put me on a handcycle for therapy. It was amazing! To be able to go fast again made me feel like I was a kid again. When I started racing with Achilles, I was given a great platform to share my faith and to inspire others to attempt the impossible.

My first races were the 2012 Chicago and Detroit marathons. At Achilles, it doesn't matter if someone takes first place or last, they care for and treat everyone the same. That's what really kept me coming back. Because when you join Achilles, you become family.

To be able to exercise, compete, do what you thought was impossible, and to do it with people just like you, is truly special.

> That is what Achilles is all about. To be able to come together with people like me is life changing.

It's important to share what you're going through and seek out others to learn from. No one was meant to walk this life alone.

I believe that God put me on that handcycle for a reason and has used the bike to help heal me. When I finish a race, people see me achieve something that was thought to be impossible. That gets them interested, and then I can share my story with them. Hopefully, they walk away from our conversation inspired to do the things for themselves they think are impossible.

I have had the support of my family and friends, of people like Dick Traum who has supported me in training and racing for years, and of mechanics, massage therapists, training partners like Alfredo de los Santos and so many more. Most importantly, I have the support of my wife, who takes care of everything when I leave for races or training. I would never have achieved the level of international success without these people.

No journey ever starts without the first step. The first time I rode a handcycle in 2010, I hurt so bad afterward that it took me a whole year to ride the bike again. I just didn't want to do it. But, when I rode it again in 2011, I told my wife that she had to make me go out and do it again the next day. I knew I was going to be sore and I wouldn't want to do it again, but I also knew I had to.

Since that second ride back in 2011, I have never stopped. You have to take the first step, and you have to have people to support you. And if you don't have that person, look me up and I will be your support person.

Tom Davis at 2018 Boston Marathon

Indeed, many of these inspired vets finish marathons and immediately ask, "What's next?" Their level of aspiration increases as they realize how limitless the possibilities are. Like me, they relish in people seeing them in a different light. They are no longer perceived as poor souls with a deficit. They are 5K finishers! They are marathon finishers! They are Ironman finishers! And they will never again regard their disability as an impediment. In fact, they will go on to carry the torch and inspire others – disabled and otherwise – to get to the start line and go the distance.

I finished Detroit on my handcycle at 2:31 and was delighted to reunite with our Achilles members after the race. Strong friendships and the smiles on every face are always highlights of events like these. Achilles provides a sense of community and a goal: completion of a collective challenge. It makes life fun. The learning experience and fellowship come from the power of the group and are among the most important factors of rehabilitation.

—————

A key ingredient of the recipe will always be our strategy. For Achilles, it was to acclimate people with disabilities into mainstream long-distance running events. I became active with Outward Bound, an international nonprofit that provides outdoor leadership programs for youth and adults, and discovered that its founder, Kurt Hahn, had a famous quote: "Disability becomes an opportunity."

With this in mind, I focused on building a community of like-minded people to form programs and events to support these disabled athletes. As Achilles progressed, it became a constant reminder that my life-changing experience was allowing me to give and receive affection. Most importantly, I had opened the doors for many other athletes such as Alfredo De Los Santos and Tom Davis to participate in mainstream events.

Another good example of a life-changing experience was the Terry Fox Race, which I referenced earlier. More than 35 years have passed since the 17-year-old basketball player Terry Fox lost his leg to cancer. The night before his surgery, his coach showed him a picture from Runner's World. It was a photograph of me at age 35 running the 1976 New York City Marathon wearing a prosthetic leg. Terry took one look at the photo and said, "If that old guy can run a marathon, I could run one every day!"

And he did. With his artificial leg, in 1980 Terry began to run across Canada to raise funds for cancer research. After he had completed 3,339 miles at the rate of 26.2 miles a day, his cancer returned and ultimately took his life. Yet his legacy and inspiration live on – not only with others, but also with me. In fact, I've participated in the Terry Fox Race more than 25 times. Races promoted in Terry's name have raised more than $715 million.

In September 1981 and 1982, I went to Toronto to fundraise for the 10K Terry Fox races. At that time, I noticed many disabled people involved as spectators, volunteers and participants. The people with disabilities were treated very well, and there was a high comfort level; there was no sense of having to hide one's disability, and there was no patronizing.

Returning from the Terry Fox runs, I wondered why we couldn't introduce running to people with disabilities in New York. I met with the president of New York Road Runners, Fred Lebow, and we developed a plan. Like me, Fred believed that running was for everyone. He fell in love with the sport on his first run, and he spent the rest of his life sharing his passion with millions of others.

With Fred's support, we sent out 1,100 flyers to people in health-related businesses and offered an eight-week program for people with disabilities. Recruiting was very difficult, but I approached it with the determination of a salesman. In our first meeting, only two people showed up. But soon we changed the program to a running club called Achilles and by the fall, six members of Achilles completed the New York City Marathon.

Achilles began to receive some media attention, and fans began to line up on event routes as our members completed their journeys. People would look once or twice and then not really notice it. The same became true of our athletes in Central Park. At first, people would notice an individual in a wheelchair or someone who was blind. Years later, such people ran unnoticed.

One year, as I was watching the marathon at 90th Street and Fifth Avenue, someone passed using a wheelchair, and another person, who was blind, ran by holding a rope. A third person passed using crutches. Just then, a mother, standing next to her teenaged son and watching all this, observed, "My goodness, this must be a dangerous sport!"

Over the next few years, Achilles expanded its numbers and added cities and even countries. By 1985, we had 25 members completing the marathon. I felt like we would run out of people with disabilities. We also had a number of Achilles stars – celebrities in their own right – with a great range of stories to tell. Our strategy was to drive expansion in every area of our organization.

In the words of Pablo Picasso, "Our goals can only be reached through a vehicle of a plan, in which we must fervently believe, and upon which we must vigorously act. There is no other route to success." Tying a clear plan to the strategy is paramount to achieving the vision. But a strategy without a plan is only an aspiration, nothing more. A plan without a strategy is a road map to somewhere, but we're not really sure where. The strategy is the starting point of a plan, and they need to be tethered together.

And so we continued to grow. In 1986, Irv Bader was responsible for the Office of Adaptive Physical Education in the New York City Board of Education. Irv would take a busload of children to Central Park where they could run, walk and wheel a short distance. We pulled together a team of disabled teenagers in a Queens high school, helped by its Adapted Physical Education teacher Bari Slatis. Several of the disabled students (under 18) were given the green light to train and run in the New York City Marathon. From these humble beginnings, the vision became a reality. This was what we like to call our "Aha" moment – helping kids develop a healthy self-image and gain confidence through running.

Today, Achilles Kids is our largest program, with more than 12,000 children participating in over 350 schools across 19 states. The children have all types of disabilities. Their goal is to run a total of 26.2 miles over the course of a school year. Awards include a T-shirt, an Achilles Kids wristband, a half marathon medal and a pair of running shoes for those who run the distance. We awarded more than 6,500 pairs of shoes in 2017, 5,000 of which were contributed by Adidas. These children – having earned a renewed sense of themselves and a fresh pair of sneakers – smile broadly and stand tall as they tell others what they accomplished.

Achilles Kids is a goal, an award and an opportunity for these young athletes to let the world know about their success. Our goal is to introduce disabled children to achievement and to a lesson that – with effort and support and tenacity – one can accomplish something many would consider impossible. Not only are Achilles Kids in better physical shape and thinking well of themselves, but they also share a glow with others who meet them and who often see halos over their heads. It's a wonderful way to pass through life.

The Terry Fox Race and our Achilles Kids constantly remind me of what people can accomplish when they have the right plan and the mindset of a motivated micro community to achieve a goal. When we formulate a solid plan, our strategy sets us on a path to achieve our vision.

From David: More Than Marathons...

Our real-world examples to this point have emphasized remarkable stories emerging from the Cigna/Achilles partnership. But the concepts we're highlighting and the importance of creating a strategy have broad applicability, regardless of life circumstance or goal.

For instance, consider Shawn King's story.

One day at work, retired Marine Staff Sergeant King and his colleagues decided to have some fun guessing one another's weight. The group consensus put Shawn's estimated weight at just over 200 pounds, and he laughed – because they were pretty accurate.

But Shawn's life was about to change dramatically and literally overnight.

The very next morning, Shawn woke up to the realization that he had gained a highly noticeable amount of weight overnight. He could barely breathe and was understandably panicked.

Shawn hurried to the emergency room, arriving, in fact, just in the nick of time.

He was quickly diagnosed with congestive heart failure and, in an ironic twist of fate, diabetes – the same disease that had contributed to his father and brother's death.

Obviously, Shawn would need a lot of care moving forward. And yet, he didn't even have a primary care physician, let alone a cardiologist for outpatient care. So, who was going to monitor him? Fortunately, before he was even discharged, Loretta Lane, a nurse at the Piedmont Clinic, and Frankie Chen, a Cigna clinical pharmacist, got involved in his treatment. They made it their mission to make sure Shawn received the care he needed.

Loretta and Frankie – who together became a micro community in support of Shawn – worked together with him to coordinate a game plan. Loretta monitored Shawn's health almost on a daily basis – lab work, vital signs, weight and so on – to evaluate how he was progressing.

A new micro community had been formed, with a goal of helping Shawn take care of his own health...quickly.

Within the context of Shawn's health, the micro community of Loretta and Frankie demonstrated how small, dedicated teams can come together to provide education, support and encouragement. They worked with Shawn to set a goal, and to support him to the point where he can now say, "Hey, I'm doing OK now. I've got this."

"A new micro community had been formed, with a goal of helping Shawn take care of his own health...quickly."

THE COURAGE TO GO FORWARD

Shawn King

Cigna Collaborative Care Customer | Georgia

In the Marines, I was always lifting weights, always running. But I wasn't fit at all; I was fit for something bad to happen. But at my job, when we were guessing each other's weight, I was sitting there basically laughing and joking with everybody.

Within 24 hours, my weight just blew up... I couldn't breathe. I was thinking "just let me make it to this hospital."

Three cardiologists came in and one said, "Yes, classic symptoms of congestive heart failure." It hit me because my older brother had just passed away in May. He was a diabetic. I lost my dad the same way.

Once I was discharged, about a day later, I received a phone call from Loretta. From that moment on, every day at 8 o'clock in the morning, the phone rang.

"Good morning, Shawn."

"Good morning, Loretta."

She really made me read labels. She would send me brochures, just educating me on the effects of not taking your meds, the effects of overindulgence.

Loretta and Frankie helped to shine a light on my good health. They really are two angels. One is great, but to have two, you can't get any better than that!

03 | Attract the Right Resources

Focus on the right resources: We rely on our people, research and development, and other resources to help us build an infrastructure to get programs off the ground and sustain them over the long term.

From Dick: The Race

It's a bright Saturday morning in Central Park. A crowd of enthusiastic fans cheer on dozens of runners – two, four eight at a time – as they pass. "Hey, you're looking good! Go! Go! Go!" Hidden in the mass of competitors, Tyler McNeil harnesses every ounce of energy to make it through the final stretch of the race. When he crosses the finish line, the cheers become an indescribable crescendo. Tyler is swept up in the celebration between the hugs and high-fives from his friends and family.

No, it's not the New York City Marathon. It's the Achilles Kids workout for disabled children around the Central Park Reservoir. Tyler was diagnosed with autism spectrum disorder (ASD) at age three. After friends introduced his mother to Achilles, he started running with our guides. Tyler trained and prepared for four months – beginning with short runs and practice with breathing and pacing techniques until he could tackle longer distances. Along the way, our volunteers and trainers made sure he had the skills and proficiency to move ahead. Now, his hard work – and the work of our Cigna/Achilles team – has paid off. Tyler is triumphant.

According to the CDC, about one-in-68 children, or 1.5 percent, was identified to have ASD based on tracking in 11 communities across the United States in 2012.

Over 12,000 children with disabilities participate in Achilles programs, and the majority of them are on the spectrum. Over the years, we've seen many of these courageous children – just like Tyler – show immediate and measured improvements in their physical and emotional health.

First, they discover that – as runners – they compare to the general population of able-bodied athletes. My 35 years of experience indicates they are frequently better runners than children who do not have special needs. All of a sudden, these autistic children realize their abilities advance them beyond the abilities of other runners. They are empowered and delighted.

A child who is nonverbal quickly realizes, "Hey, I am really good at this." Many of them aspire to become professional runners. They say, "OK, I've finally found something that I can do better than most other people. What's next?"

One of the greatest obstacles for children with autism is that they become anxious, their hearts pound and they get butterflies in their stomach in social settings. Once they're running though, people are telling them, "You're great. You're terrific. Congratulations." Running encourages these children to socialize with others, leading to improved levels of self-confidence.

Parents have told me how Achilles events have helped their sons and daughters make enormous improvements in their outlook and disposition. They are applying their energy in a productive way – toward achievement.

Better physical health, enhanced social skills and improved cognition. That's the spirit of our mobilized micro community, drawing on its spirit and resources to inspire its members.

My story about Tyler took place years ago. Today, Tyler is in his late twenties and has been with Achilles for about 20 years. He started with Achilles Kids and now he's competing in marathons and triathlons, inspiring dozens of others along the way. While Tyler has a limited vocabulary, he is a true champion and superstar among his peers. At 6'4", he stands out in a crowd. One could easily mistake him for an Olympic athlete. When he leaps into the water with the dexterity of an Olympic swimmer, college coaches watch in amazement, hoping to recruit their next superstar. His mother found Achilles and Tyler has discovered who he's meant to be.

Through funding from the Cigna Foundation, research has produced evidence that running boosts overall quality of life –

and for children with autism, it can be a significant supplement to traditional therapies and medical procedures.

I believe that in the future, when we treat autism, it is possible we'll recognize that the most valuable part of a child's development is the support a micro community can provide to encourage participation in mainstream events. In our case it's running.

————

As we follow our recipe, we find that dedicated resources support the vision of our micro community. Whether it's Achilles or a larger accomplishment on the corporate level, there's a massive support system required to make things happen. Within our micro community, every component of the infrastructure – whether human or financial – serves as an essential part of the equation.

It has been said that hard work and talent can make anything happen. We have seen the results of true talent first-hand.

A big part of our micro community is volunteers. Larry Sillen, the first Achilles volunteer, is a professional photographer and a retired PR executive. He photographed the first Achilles race and has taken more than two million pictures of our athletes over the course of 35 years. He finds immense joy in giving our members pictures of race highlights and significant moments in their lives - all free of charge.

Andy Ashwell has been an Achilles volunteer for more than 20 years. He attends our workouts twice a week, every week, and volunteers over 100 times during the course of a year. To date, he has logged more than 6,000 hours training and attending practices and races. He pairs our volunteer walkers with slower Achilles members. He also takes care of a special racing wheelchair for one of our members with cerebral palsy, Bill Reilly. Achilles is Andy's extended family.

A few years ago, before a two-mile race was set to begin in Central Park, Cyril Charles, one of our visually impaired athletes, needed a guide. George Hirsch was standing near the front of the pack preparing to start, and I asked him if he could help. George was eager to finish the race in under 12 minutes, and he had trained long and hard for this moment. But instead, he agreed to run with Cyril, and George did all he could to keep up with the blind athlete who was nearly three decades his junior. The two crossed the finish line in 11 minutes and 52 seconds. George admits that he would never have broken his personal record without Cyril by his side.

Larry, Andy and George are just a few examples of the capable, motivated and talented partners who embody our support system. It's not a vague, theoretical support. It's real, tangible and personal.

Perhaps Zoe Heineman expressed it best when she sent an email to her fellow Achilles members after completing a race:

> *Dear Super Heroes,*
>
> *I am filled with gratitude and love at this moment. It's thanks to you that I am here, enjoying this feeling of accomplishment today.*
>
> *Wow...how do you thank someone who has taken you from the fear of success to the joy of success? Simply by telling them and saying thank you seems like a good place to start.*
>
> *Each of you has guided me in a race and/or coached me to participate and finish a BHAG (big hairy achievable goal). More than that, you fundamentally encouraged me. That means more than I can tell you. Thank you, from the bottom of my heart.*
>
> *This morning I completed my 2nd ever Achilles Sprint distance Triathlon with 10 other Achilles athletes at Chelsea Piers Indoor Triathlon. What a joy! I can hardly believe I did it!*
>
> *We ask ourselves "What if?" and we learn what is possible. Come join me in another race this year. I would like to share this joy with you again.*
>
> *Happy Sunday wherever you are! I raise a glass to you.*
>
> *Hugs,*
> *Zoe*

Our actions provide a window into what is in our hearts. We give others hope. "The greatness of a community is most accurately measured by the compassionate actions of its members," Coretta Scott King wrote. The power for change through motivated and talented volunteers such as ours can move individuals, pick them up and set them on a course to personal fulfillment.

Whether we are focused on volunteerism or another endeavor, the more committed our people are to the purpose, the more sustainable our support system will be.

One of our Freedom Team members in the Achilles Houston Chapter, Rick, penned this note to the director of the Achilles Freedom Team, Janet Patton, after he completed the 2018 Boston Marathon.

> *Good morning!*
>
> *Made it home and finally stopped shivering.*
>
> *This was the most difficult race I have been in but aside from the shivering it was a real adventure! I am now ready for anything...*
>
> *I have never mentioned this...I don't often talk about challenges but since I got out of the service I have had difficulty with crowds... not anonymous crowds so much...but crowds of people I am familiar with.....at times I just need quiet.*
>
> *I have noticed over the 10 races with the Freedom Team that in the last couple I am becoming more comfortable with being around the group. I don't know if I can describe what this is like for me after almost half a century behind a wall that only opened slightly at times.*
>
> *You have allowed and helped make it possible for me to do what no other person has been able to do.*
>
> *I just wanted you to know you have made a friend for life......a life you have helped make better.*
>
> *Rick*

Even during more modest events such as those for Achilles Kids, people are generally unaware of the sacrifices made to prepare and build up to the actual day. It really does take a village, and we create hundreds of little villages – with an enormous number of potential volunteers and dedicated resources – to make it possible for athletes like Rick to reach their goals.

Helene Hines and Ted Rogers are two talented and generous individuals who have helped Achilles achieve its vision and become a vibrant and growing organization.

Helene has multiple sclerosis (MS) and is the founder of the Achilles handcycle program. She completed several marathons as a runner, beating her husband, George, and son, Brian, in the Boston Marathon with a four-hour time. She also competed in the Comrades in Durban, a 56-mile race over the mountains of South Africa. When Helene's MS ran its course, she purchased a handcycle wheelchair and began to compete with her new device. Her times were world class, finishing marathons well under two hours. When I had my knee replaced in 2000, she gave me an old one to use. Thanks to her gift, I had a new sport and a renewed spirit to compete.

Ted Rogers is a founding Achilles board member. His favorite volunteering experience was in 1995 when he accompanied our founding board chair, Trisha Meili, in the New York City Marathon and finished in four-and-a-half hours. Ted has also volunteered internationally, running as an Achilles volunteer accompanying Eddie Pazarecki in the Warsaw Marathon.

Helene and Ted have helped Achilles achieve its vision and become a vibrant and growing organization. Bonnie Marks, another volunteer and member of our Achilles board, has also made a significant contribution with her work at The Rusk Institute of Rehabilitation Medicine at New York University. Bonnie and her team worked with marathon runners with traumatic brain injuries and gave us enormous insight into how these athletes improved cognitively in a manner that's never been seen before.

If your vision is clear, resources will arrive in droves. For instance, we are always caught off guard to see so many people apply to serve as volunteers and guides for Achilles events. During our two-week application period for the New York City Marathon and the preliminary workouts, we had far more applicants than spots on our team. Why? Because many of our volunteers and guides have described working a marathon as the most anticipated day in their lives, and their passion to help others is truly remarkable.

Within our micro community, there are hundreds of dedicated volunteers, true givers who inspire our members and help us move our strategy forward.

Mary Bryant, who continued to volunteer, wanted to run the marathon with her brother, Don, who was paralyzed from the neck down. Mary – an accomplished runner and model – devised a way for Don to activate a battery-operated wheelchair by moving his head backwards. A replacement battery at the 13-mile mark helped him go the distance and complete the marathon. Don said it was the best day of his life.

We have built a support system of talented people who are well-equipped to address setbacks by helping our members gain self-confidence and approach problems with a can-do attitude. They have helped hundreds of disabled individuals pick themselves up and overcome their insecurities at every point along the journey.

They have discovered the joy of giving. Our talented partners make a big difference and their selfless attitudes are the lifeblood of the success of our strategy.

Beyond talent, we draw from research and development and seek funding to support our infrastructure. For example, in a study funded by the Cigna Foundation, researchers from Achilles and New York Medical College measured the quantitative and qualitative effects of the Achilles running program on restrictive/ repetitive behaviors, social interaction, social communication, emotional responses and cognitive style in 94 students with autism across five schools.

This real-world, "natural setting" study was among the largest conducted to date. Results showed profound and statistically significant improvements in key areas such as fitness markers and communication behaviors, further validating the team's hypothesis that a vigorous school-based exercise program has the potential to positively impact physical, social, academic and emotional factors for students with higher levels of impairment.

Our employees, members and volunteers also actively participate in various fundraising activities – such as the Achilles annual fundraising dinner – and sponsorship for participation in Achilles events. We also have been blessed with creative ideas. Two, for example, were generated by Achilles hand cyclists and marathoners David Greenstein who has MS and Neil Mellon who, in his eighties, is arthritic. While working out together, their question was, "How can we help grow this great program?" The answer: We need more handcycles. David and Neil donated 25, helping us make a great leap forward. Next they asked, "What else can I do?" The suggestion, an annual Lakin Challenge. Each year David and Neil match up to $50,000 in donations. Their generosity supports our handcycle program, which is the largest in the nation and most likely the world.

Beyond her work as a member and volunteer, Mary Bryant also has been a significant fundraiser, contributor and donor. We also have corporate donors such as General Motors, which sponsors the Detroit Marathon and our Freedom Team members over the past several years.

From David: The Importance of Connectors

In April 2018, I was in Arizona with members of the Cigna team for a meeting with several physician leaders. After the meeting ended, one of the younger gentlemen (who was clearly in top physical form) approached me and said, "Can I ask you a question on a different topic? This Boston Marathon thing that I read about. I've been a triathlete for a long time. I'm over trying to get faster. I want to make a difference. How do I do that?"

This is another example of finding the right resource with the right mindset. The young man's frame of mind wasn't, "I want to run the Boston Marathon." He had already transitioned from the self-satisfaction of racing and getting faster to "I'm looking for a different purpose. And I want that." That is what I call a leveragability point – where we can leverage our resources. And I said, "I'll bridge you across that." Now, we have a physician leader in a large hospital system in a major metropolitan area, who emotionally wants to do it.

I guarantee that if you emotionally give in to something like this and you experience it, you're going to ask yourself rhetorically, "How do I give more? How do I leverage myself more?"

So, you can provide support in a variety of ways. You can give your talent. You can give your time. You can give your money. Whether small, medium or larger in scope, we need to be mindful of the resources – time, talent or funding – that we need to achieve our vision.

When we look at The ChildObesity180 initiative we see yet another example of how the right resources can make a big difference. While many corporations give generously to philanthropic programs from a financial perspective – which I certainly applaud –it is more important for us in some cases to give time, or skills or resources. Here we have executives, leaders and volunteers with diverse skill sets sharing their expertise and time for the greater good. The dedication and compassion of this micro community left me in awe of how individuals can come together and give their time and energy to a singular vision and make a huge impact.

As the scope of the mission expands, so too must the variety of resources to tackle the challenge. In the context of the recipe, cooking for yourself may mean experimenting with the recipe and taking more chances with fewer ingredients. Preparing a recipe for your family or someone else may call for a different dynamic based on their tastes and desires. Cooking for 1,000 people most likely would require help from others. The size of the meal will necessitate more or fewer resources, a larger kitchen or several appliances.

Likewise, the size of the micro community will require connecting to various sources that are out there and available, including finding likeminded individuals with resources to contribute – from their time to talent to dollars. When Achilles taps into the Cigna Foundation and its mission, we see a leveraged effect that creates more micro communities.

As we move from situational to more sustainable micro communities, we see the value in leveraging our achievements. If we simply look for ways to fundraise around our initiative to get it off the ground, we're taking the hardest route to success. We'll slow scaling down and slow leveraging down if all we think about is our funding sources.

Conversely, if we focus on attracting the right resources to drive a level of alignment within, we'll create a more sustainable resource of like-minded partners. The key is to spend time finding the right people such as Larry Sillen or Andy Ashwell or those who give their time to the ChildObesity180 initiative and who are mentally and emotionally aligned with the vision. We can leverage this to build more sustainable communities.

The Cigna Foundation aligned with Achilles' purpose, which goes far beyond, "buy a table at my event." That's a one-and-done where the check is written and we can walk away. Within a more sustainable mindset, we rent-to-own, paying it forward with our time and talent rather than simply focusing on the money.

Finding and aligning with the right resources is paramount to the success of any micro community – whether small, medium or large. Oftentimes, we only think about the sustainability of resources – people, skills and money – required for larger-scale initiatives and we lose sight of the enormous potential a smaller-scale program can have. As we saw when Melissa Wilcox started Philly Achilles, smaller situational micro communities require very few resources.

As we scale toward medium and larger sustainable micro communities, we can identify more robust resources and build our infrastructures accordingly. Within the context of the overall vision, these resources help to sustain and perpetuate the micro community. But let's not think the only way to make a difference is to create some grandiose thing, as opposed to a more modest aspiration that can impact one person, one day at a time. More often than not, a humble act and just your time can be a powerful gift to anyone who needs a helping hand. This is where it all begins.

Another lesson from my meeting in Arizona relates to becoming the living and breathing representation of your micro community. In his book *The Tipping Point,* Malcolm Gladwell describes Connectors as people who link us up with the world. These people possess a special gift for bringing the world together. In our experience, micro communities are filled with Connectors who cultivate networks of like-minded people. We value the ability to connect and find ways to bridge an individual's vision with a recipe for achievement.

Nadine McNeil crossing
the Verrazano Bridge at
New York City Marathon

Achillies Family member
at 2018 Boston Marathon

Antonio Martinez is neck
and neck at the 2014 NYRR
Fifth Avenue Mile

04 | Execute to Achieve the Plan

Once we define our aspirations and create a strategy,
the difference between success and failure is our ability
to execute to achieve the plan.

From David: Make Your Plan Work for You

After he completed the 2015 Boston Marathon, Cedric King
asked me if I would run with his friend and fellow Freedom
Team member Stefan LeRoy in his first race. Stefan had lost both
of his feet two years before when he stepped on an IED while
carrying one of his fallen comrades on a stretcher to a helicopter in
Afghanistan. He came to accept his disability as part of his life and
never viewed it as a limitation.

I ran as a guide for Stefan at the Walt Disney World Half
Marathon on Jan. 8, 2016.

Almost immediately after we crossed the finish line, Stefan
turned to me and said, "Do you think I could do a full marathon?"

I told him yes, but I didn't say more because we were still caught
up in the emotion of his great half-marathon finish.

"I want to run Boston," he said immediately. I was tired. It was
January. Boston was in April, three months away.

So I told him, "You're on a high. Don't make that decision now."

Stefan's response underscored his renewed confidence. "Cedric
told me I should do the Boston Marathon," he said.

"Take the rest of the month to sit back, think and reflect,"
I suggested. "You can do it, but don't decide now. On January
31, call me and tell me yes or no. If it's yes, tell me why."

The text came in late January. It was Stefan, who had a well-
thought-out argument why he wanted to run the Boston
Marathon – not why Cedric wanted him to do it, but why he
wanted to do it. As soon as he made his case, I thought, "all
right, I'm all in." Failure is not an option for Stefan or me.

Throughout his training for Boston, Stefan and I were in different locations – unable to work out together. So, I never had an opportunity to train with him side by side. But we made sure we communicated through texts throughout his training. He had set a goal, and now he had a plan and needed a level of commitment to achieve it.

Finally, it was race day in Boston: April 18, 2016. I was prepared to support Stefan along the way. My role was to make sure he was hydrated and had the proper nutrition because he'd never experienced a run for that duration. If he took the half-marathon logic to a full marathon, it wouldn't work. With a full marathon, there were multiple logistics to consider, from hydration to nutrition, the pacing and the mindset needed. It all requires a dedicated support system for that longer distance. Stefan had the will to do it, but we needed to augment his raw determination with the tangible means to execute and achieve his vision.

We all execute in the best manner we know, adapting and adjusting to the plan. Everyone takes their own approach. For example, Cedric King preferred to place his arms over my shoulders for leverage as we went up hills. My pulling allowed him to recover just a bit. But Stefan was not comfortable with this technique and instead would prefer my hand on the small of his back, pushing while extending my free hand for him to grasp onto for balance.

We all learn to adjust and adopt!

For Stefan, the key was also taking the time to reflect and then dig deep inside to determine what's really important to him and why it's important, and then crystallizing it. Because people will say, "I want to do that because somebody else did it." Well, if that's the full extent of your rationale, you're not really committed to it and you're not going to execute. Not really. It all comes back to why do you want to do it? Find the why and you'll discover the how.

David Cordani, Stefan LeRoy and Katie
Smith at Walt Disney World® Marathon
Weekend presented by Cigna
©Disney

THE COURAGE TO GO FORWARD

Stefan LeRoy

Ret. Sergeant, U.S. Army | Florida

I knew a full marathon was going to be an enormous challenge for me. Yet, I was determined. And so I surrounded myself with the support I needed to accomplish this goal. I relied heavily on David, who worked with my fiancée Katie to create a training schedule to make sure I was putting in the miles before the actual run in Boston. To say that he made the training manageable and easier for me is an understatement.

David is exactly what a supportive friend and guide should be, constantly going above and beyond expectations so I could concentrate on the challenge in front of me. He also knew the course like the back of his hand, so he told me where we should take wider turns, where there is a hole in the ground and when I should anticipate upcoming obstacles.

Achilles and David have become like a family to me and just knowing there are others like me out there accomplishing goals makes it so much easier. The inspiration I gain from this community is just fantastic and it motivates me to encourage others who are facing similar challenges. When others see us racing on handcycles, racing in wheelchairs or while wearing prosthetics, they realize they can go out and do it, too. That's the great impact of Achilles. All of those training rides and runs in between races create a sense within the community that anyone can do this — anyone who is determined and puts their mind to it.

> It's just an awesome feeling when an athlete tells you they are going to start running because they saw you run.

When I hear that from a disabled person, it means so much more because I know firsthand how difficult and overwhelming it was for me to get started. But the biggest reward for me is to know that I helped another person realize they can overcome any challenge they face. I encourage them by saying, "You can do this. We've got you."

Cedric King was one of the athletes who initially told me I could run farther and do it sooner than I thought I could. He helped me get through the physical and the psychological part of it, to believe a marathon was possible. Now, I hope that I am paying it forward.

Whether you have a disability or not, the key is to put yourself out there, break it down into small increments and say, "Hey, I'm going to do this." And once you do it, then say, "Hey, I did it and it wasn't really that tough." Then, you go out and do it again.

Stefan LeRoy at 2018 Boston Marathon

Stefan's road to Boston was baked into the recipe. It began with the vision of what he wanted to achieve. Next, he created a strategy and found support. Then he went at it with focus and determination. Rinse, repeat; rinse, repeat; rinse, repeat. That's the execution part of the strategy.

It all came back to reaffirming his goal and asking, "Do I really want this? Why do I want it?"

Whatever we pursue – whether it's talking to somebody about their athletic pursuits, their career or their academic interests – needs to reflect our character, personal goals, persona and expectations. Often, an individual may project what's right for another, but that may not necessarily be right for this person.

The pursuit of a marathon may not have been appropriate for Stefan. "Should I run Boston or not?" was a question only he could answer. As his guide, I needed to be fully engaged and emotionally vested in Stefan's vision and understand the ramifications of his goal. The spirit of supporting another as a selfless servant, getting into his head, was paramount for me.

Whether it's one person or a team, we initially think, "I don't know how the hell it's going to happen, but it's going to happen." Then, we execute on the recipe and make it happen. If you want it badly enough – if you have the passion – you'll find a way to execute and do it. I truly believe that.

Having a relentless attitude to achieve your plan has an effect on others, and your success begets more success. When you find the will – the resolve to achieve your goal – you may not know exactly how, but your faith in the process means, "I'm not going to be beaten. This is not going to defeat me."

Looking back, three years ago Stefan needed encouragement and support to help him execute on his vision. There was doubt and uncertainty. Today, he is self-motivated, self-driven and he doesn't need much encouragement. I'll check in with him from time to time. But he is filled mostly with confidence, curiosity and some episodic fear like everybody else has.

That's only human, because you don't have to have an amputation to have that episodic experience. People can have that experience for a variety of negative reasons – being a cancer survivor, losing a job, getting divorced or learning a sibling was killed. When life changes, we have every reason to stop.

Here we saw Stefan find his willpower and start up again, getting on with his life.

For all of us, happily ever after means a life with all its idiosyncrasies: good days, bad days, complex days, challenging days. With the help of others, more is within our control than when we first thought, "Nothing's in my control." Because many times people who face a life-changing experience start from the perspective of, "My life as I know it is over."

In Stefan's case, I tried to encourage him to make sure he really thought deeply about the daring goal he was about to set. We went back to the early part of the recipe because when you pursue something that's hard, it's going to be hard for a while. But if you really want it, you'll be driven to plow through those chapters. You don't really want to keep working toward your goal when the headwinds blow and the barriers come and the unexpected events happen. It's easier to exhale and say, "Not meant to be."

By the way, the day I told Stefan "No," I was certain he could do it. His strength was palpable. But he had to believe he could do it. That was the whole notion of the psychology of it. Because I knew that training for a marathon was going to be a lot harder than anything he ever did.

This is why the recipe goes back to the person who sets the goal and really, deeply wants to achieve it. Because that passion will drive them out of their comfort zone and open them up to help from others. Both are imperative. Because if you think "I got it," you're not going to be open to outside assistance. It's important to understand the value of a support system and the need to execute on the plan.

Bryan Ott learned first-hand about the importance of being open to outside assistance, and the value of a strong support system, after ignoring his personal wellness for far too long.

Highly active while growing up in Kennesaw, Georgia, he played baseball and football and participated in many other physical activities. After moving to Atlanta as an adult, however, he became less active, and far less mindful of his diet and lifestyle. His weight increased and general health deteriorated.

Along the way, Daleis Hamrick, an embedded care coordinator at Piedmont Clinic, entered his life. Embedded care coordinators are clinicians who support patient care and plan development.

Cigna works closely with embedded care coordinators through its collaborative program with health care providers to fill these roles, providing them with patient-specific information to help them coordinate care, contact patients at risk for chronic disease and to help patients resolve clinical gaps in care.

As Daleis reviewed Bryan's Cigna-provided health information as part of her routine monitoring, she quickly determined that Bryan's elevated A1C level, among other health challenges, made Bryan a prime candidate for significant future health problems.

"Once his blood sugar was controlled and he did feel better, that was his turning point," Daleis recalled. "When Bryan tells me what I've done for him, I just take it as part of my job. I just gave him the information. He's got to do it."

In this equation, Cigna embraced its role as an enabler, helping to connect and mobilize its health care professional partners and customers.

With this collaborative care arrangement, we see a clearly defined vision, a strategy and a plan of action built around talented professionals. Once again, the recipe goes back to the person who sets the goal and commits to achieving it. In Bryan's case, he was driven out of his comfort zone and opened to getting help from Daleis and Cigna. The support system was in place to help him execute on his plan.

"In this equation, Cigna embraced its role as an enabler, helping to connect and mobilize its health care professional partners and customers."

PROFILES IN COURAGE

THE COURAGE TO GO FORWARD

Bryan Ott

Cigna Collaborative Care Customer | Georgia

I didn't realize that I didn't really feel okay.

I thought that diabetes only happened to older people. I thought, "I'm too young. I'm only 30. I can't have diabetes."

When Daleis started calling, I saw her as kind of a thorn in my side. I guess at one point, though, it became, "Wait, maybe I need to spend more time listening to her."

I knew I could be living better and that I should be living better.

Cigna also helped me in other areas of my life. Not just doctor's office visits; it was counseling, it was anything that affected my daily life. I don't feel like I'm only a customer, I feel like I'm an actual person.

Daleis was there when I needed her. She's the star, because she was the motivator.

I feel like now I'm adding time on to my life instead of subtracting it from my life. I may have diabetes but diabetes doesn't have me.

05 | Overcome Obstacles

No matter how foolproof our recipe may be, we should always expect obstacles, setbacks and a few stumbles along the way — and be prepared to adjust accordingly.

From David: Determination and Feedback Required

Matias Ferreira is a U.S. Marine veteran who lost both legs and broke his pelvis in Afghanistan at age 19 after stepping on an IED. A handsome man who had a modeling career before he went to Afghanistan, Lance Corporal Ferreira is a charismatic individual. I had the privilege of guiding him in the 2012 Walt Disney World Half Marathon – just a little more than a year after his devastating accident – and have witnessed his spirit and perseverance first hand.

Lance Corporal Ferreira was trying to find his identity. From the start, I could tell that brotherhood – a sense of being a part of a team – was important to him. As a Marine, he was part of one of the most elite military units serving his country. When he returned from the war, he played softball with wounded veterans – another exclusive team. Ultimately, he found a job with the International Union of Operating Engineers on Long Island. He never thought he'd be a welder, but the sense of brotherhood was important to him, and he loved it.

Ultimately, Matias set his sights on yet another elite team. He wanted be a police officer and serve his community. The vision was set, but it was highly unlikely for a double amputee. Logic would tell us it wasn't achievable.

He pursued his dream regardless. He tried, failed. Tried, failed. Tried, failed. He couldn't pass the physical test – running two miles at a minimum pace – because he had to do it on his "regular" prosthetics, not on his J legs (different than regular prosthetics, these J legs, or running blades, are specially designed to help make faster running speeds possible).

Matias kept preparing for his physical test the same way he prepared for every other running event. But up to this point, every event he completed had more of an endurance aspect. This test had a speed aspect. We had to break it down to train for track workouts. For Matias, this was what we refer to as a "fast twitch fiber" event and I had to explain to him what fast twitch fibers were versus slow twitch fibers. He had to understand the dynamic of lactic acid buildup and what happened to his body when he stimulated his fast twitch fibers. We developed a more complex training program – doing reps with slow recoveries and laps around the track.

We reviewed Matias' strategy and addressed the obstacles. He had to modify his training regimen so he could become oriented around speed work with his prosthetics. This was a totally different way of training, and it was clear just how frustrating and grueling it was. But he refused to give up.

At one point, I can remember speaking with him on the phone after one of his training sessions, hanging up and thinking, "How are we going to get there?"

He failed again.

Then he had to take the feedback. I asked him how his workouts were going, breaking his performance into smaller parts to determine his progress. We adjusted his workouts, and I could see his rate of progression.

Mentally and physically, there were obstacles to surmount. I knew his willpower was in the right place, but I felt pangs in my stomach when I thought about the academic portion of the exam, as well as what the last 600 yards of the two miles were going to feel like physically and mentally.

The initial strategy got him 80 percent of the way to his vision. Many people would say, "Well, that's a huge victory." It was, but it wasn't huge enough. So, we went at it again. Honest, interactive feedback along the way was mission-critical. Our objective was really clear, and we just needed to modify our strategy and effectively execute to achieve the goal.

After months of setbacks, adjustments and hard work, Matias had completed his journey. He finished the course and made the cutoff time! He graduated from the academy side by side with able-bodied candidates and became the first double amputee full-time police officer in the country. He was sworn in with a group of 58 other officers and was elected as their class president.

Matias was ecstatic when he shared the great news, "We did it!"

In fact, he did it. I was astonished and delighted at the same time, of course. Astonished because, on some level, I didn't think it was possible. Delighted because I knew how important it was for him. Even though we know the recipe works, it still never ceases to amaze me that someone with the persistence and dedication to follow a plan and overcome obstacles can truly accomplish anything, even something seemingly impossible. Because we know how difficult and how important achieving something can be, the magnitude of the achievement when someone finally accomplishes it can be overwhelming, as I experienced firsthand.

I remember telling my wife how excited I was for Matias and how fulfilling it was for me. I asked him to send me pictures of his first day on the job, and he sent several selfies – in his uniform, sitting in a police cruiser and even ... sitting on a motorcycle? He said, "This will be cool. A pic of me on the bike."

Seeing his pictures was a "pinch me" moment, and they will forever remain on my phone and in my heart. As my Cigna colleagues know, I can be subdued when it comes to celebrating success. But this was a huge success, and I'm still wowed by it – overjoyed that Matias was able to achieve his goal. Because, all along the way, everything pointed to how it shouldn't have happened. It's a good reinforcement of our recipe.

––––––––

Within the context of our recipe, we need to have frequent and honest feedback to overcome any obstacles and adjust the strategy en route to realize our vision. Matias' story reminds us that things happen – expectedly and unexpectedly – that can fuel the journey, slow it down or bump it off its course.

Often, we react to a setback with a thought like, "I knew I couldn't" or "I told you so." Or, "I knew it would be hard and it's harder than I thought." Lack of confidence and conceding to inevitable pitfalls and self-destruction can lead to paralysis through analysis. Left to our own devices, we may excuse ourselves and forego the journey.

Those who have the willpower and the determination rise above obstacles and do whatever it takes to work hard and prepare for the journey. But there is another characteristic that successful people like Matias have that sets them apart: They absolutely love what they are doing.

If you want to become a great golfer, you had better love the game of golf. If you want to become an elite firefighter, you had better love climbing stairs, dragging hoses, carrying equipment, raising ladders and searching for and rescuing others. If you want to become the all-time best shooter in the NBA, you had better love the hard work and intense preparation and be ready to shoot an ungodly number of shots every day.

Basketball fans arrive to Golden State Warrior games over an hour before tip-off just to watch Stephen Curry put on one of the biggest shows in the league: his pre-game routine. He takes about 105 or 110 shots, from three-pointers to scoop shots and runners, with his right and left hands, and practices catch-and-shoot shots. Move, shoot, repeat. Move, shoot, repeat.

As Stephen puts it, "If you take time to realize what your dream is and what you really want in life – no matter what it is, whether it's sports or in other fields – you have to realize that there is always work to do, and you want to be the hardest working person in whatever you do, and you put yourself in a position to be successful. And you have to have a passion about what you do."

Too often, we perceive meaningful accomplishments such as Stephen's as something that comes easy – attributable to sheer talent. But as the writer Stephen King has said, "Talent is cheaper than table salt. What separates the talented individual from the successful one is a lot of hard work." The good old-fashioned hard work part of the equation is all too often lost in the finished product. From the outside looking in, we don't realize the amount of sweat equity that successful people put in relative to pursuit of their goal.

Ben Simmons at the Lido Beach Triathlon

THE COURAGE TO GO FORWARD

If the goal is worth pursuing, you need to be willing to do the hard work and love what you are doing.

As I also witnessed with Matias, when we work with others who are more skilled, or have been through the experience before us, it accelerates our growth. Stephen Curry's father, Dell, was a great NBA shooter for the Charlotte Hornets and taught his son to play with the pros. He built Stephen's confidence and skill set by introducing him to the greatest players in the league. The experience was likely humbling for him along the way. We need to be prepared to be humbled and somewhat frustrated through the process, constantly reminding ourselves why we are doing it, always circling back to reaffirm our goal and relying on the expertise of others.

Regardless of your aspirational goal – whether it's running a marathon in under three hours, getting a Ph.D. or becoming a concert violinist – ask yourself: Do I really want to achieve it? Pure desire can be a great motivator, because the amount of work you'll need to get there is going to be off the charts. At a minimum, if you're not willing to take feedback and ask experts for advice, you're going to extend your journey longer than it has to be. The worst-case scenario is that you'll never achieve your goal. If you're willing to take feedback – including feedback from others and reflecting on your past performance – to make adjustments, you will achieve your goal.

With this in mind, I have three pieces of important advice:

1. Be deeply reflective, thoughtful and fully committed to the goal you have set – aspirational as it may be. Because you're going to find yourself getting knocked back on your heels over and over and over.

2. Ask experts for help. Successful people or stubborn people tend not to ask. Leverage others.

3. Take the feedback and adjust. If you keep doing the same thing and saying, "I'm going to try harder but I'm going to do it the same way," you're going to get a similar outcome.

People typically become experts precisely because they failed on the path to becoming successful. Tap into their wisdom.

That wisdom is scar tissue that manifests itself over time from experiences.

Yes, you have to want it and, yes, you have to be willing to do the work. But you also have to be willing to ask for help, take feedback and make adjustments along the way. Life is about adjusting.

In the nascent days of airline travel – before autopilot and GPS – when flights veered off course, pilots would manually make small micro-adjustments to keep the plane headed in the right direction. If they waited too long to adjust their route, they would find themselves far from their destination, requiring them to make more wide-ranging adjustments.

Why do we fail? In most cases, we thought the goal was clear to everybody and there was alignment around it, but there really wasn't. We thought the communications were clear, but they really weren't. As a result, we were too slow to make adjustments along the way and by the time we made adjustments, we were too far off track. Then, there is no other choice than to reload and start over.

From a business standpoint, we can also experience plenty of failings or misfires. Business failings are most commonly borne out of a few reasons. First, the vision was unclear and generated a lack of alignment. Second, communications were unclear and didn't enable or encourage the best elements of the organization to come forward. Or third, there weren't enough micro-adjustments made along the way.

How we approach the journey, make adjustments and persevere through setbacks is as important to our development as achieving the goal itself.

Let's also not gloss over the importance of the fear factor.

Those who set goals, or even aspire to goals, often find a way to eliminate the barriers simply out of fear. Was Matias fearful? No way. But fear of failure can be a big restraint. For every individual with the tenacity to succeed, there are dozens who justify the myriad reasons why they've never pursued their goals.

First, there's always tomorrow. If something is perceived to be difficult or challenging, the procrastinators recognize there's always a first day to embark on whatever they want to achieve. But, if they perpetually delay the first day until some hypothetical tomorrow, there will never be a first day. Human nature has the ability to rationalize fear in perpetuity.

In the words of Nelson Mandela, "I learned that courage was not the absence of fear, but the triumph over it."

If you want something badly, the fear of failure can be a phenomenal motivator. If you know how to face and harness your fear, it could be a source of courage to overcome any paralysis. I can remember training days when it was pouring rain outside, and my wife saw me pulling on my shorts and asked, "What are you doing?" I said, "I'm going to do a 100-mile bike ride today." Bug-eyed, she said, "It's a disaster out there." I would explain, "It could be a disaster on the day of the race, too, and mentally, I'll be ready for it."

Fear motivates us to push ourselves beyond limits, regardless of the weather or any other excuse we can invent. The challenge can become a motivator to help us overcome any obstacle that stands in our way.

06 | Expand and Grow

Just as recipes evolve when they are passed down through generations or modified with healthier ingredients, our basic recipe allows us to make improvements to broaden and expand the vision with new opportunities across more micro communities.

From Dick: Endless Possibilities

Over the years, Achilles has expanded and grown into seven core programs:

- The New York City Chapter
- New York City-based affiliates
- National and International Chapters
- Achilles Kids
- The Freedom Team
- The Marathon Tour, including the New York City Marathon
- The Hope & Possibility Four-Miler

The New York City Chapter includes several programs under the direction of Michael Anderson: the core Achilles Program, which meets twice a week and races once a month; the Tri Achilles Team, a program for triathletes; the Handcycle Program; the Friedman Diabetes program and the program for patients at Rusk Institute who have traumatic brain injuries. There are also kayak, tennis, and females with disabilities programs, and partnership with Odyssey House (an addiction rehabilitation organization) to introduce its residents undergoing substance-abuse treatment to running.

The National Chapters under the direction of Ellie Cox include 15 programs in various cities, including Madison, Wis.; Palm

Beach, Fla.; Nashville; Pittsburgh; Philadelphia; Los Angeles; Denver and Boston, plus several affiliates.

Achilles International chapters today have members in more than 70 countries around the world, including major chapters in Canada, Colombia, Russia, New Zealand and Poland, to name just a few. Gerle Shagdar, the coordinator of these international chapters, transformed our Mongolian chapter from just a few members to hundreds of members today, with the second-largest global participation in our Hope & Possibility Race. Gerle recently traveled to Japan to celebrate its first Hope & Possibility race.

The Freedom Team, under the guidance of founder Mary Bryant, Janet Patton and Joe Traum, consists of more than 1,000 recently wounded veterans recruited from Armed Forces hospitals to compete in long-distance running.

Finally, there is the Hope & Possibility Four-Miler, directed by Toby Tanser. We recently changed the distance from five to four miles, to encourage even more participants. Taking place in Central Park, the race is celebrating its 16th year and features disabled athletes in a mainstream race with able-bodied athletes. Runners participate and win several prizes, including small cash awards. In 2003, when Trisha ran the race for the first time, she guided former New York Gov. David Paterson, a blind athlete who became the chairman of the board of Achilles.

The Four-Miler is a place where blind, ambulatory disabled, amputees and wheelchair users can win in their divisions and celebrate their achievements. Celebrities and public figures such as Prince Harry, Cindy and Meghan McCain, Heather Mills and comedian Jon Stewart have also joined us for the event.

A few years ago, we increased the number of chapters in the states and established new ones across the globe, taking advantage of new opportunities. Our strategy was much like planting seeds in a field – we could either plant a few at a time or spread them across a large area and hope that some would take root.

Today, many of our international chapters and athletes join us for the New York City Marathon, a huge draw for many of our athletes. Tran Trong Cao, a veteran of the North Vietnamese army with a below-the-knee artificial leg, once ran the marathon with Jerry Chmielak, a West Point graduate and Vietnam veteran. Decades before, they were at war. Now, they were a team.

The Norway chapter head, Ketil Moe, had cystic fibrosis and encouraged the Norwegian athletes Grete Waitz and Johann Koss to run the New York City Marathon. Each year, there was a race in Ketil's hometown of Lillesand in southern Norway, integrating able-bodied and disabled athletes. Every finisher was awarded a medal by five-time Olympic Gold medal winner Koss. Ketil Moe became a hero in his home country, penning a book and bonding with his fellow runners from Norway.

A large group of Achilles runners come to the New York race from South Africa. One member, Incele Mosiana, is an amputee runner who received an artificial leg through Achilles and ran a marathon, returned home and helped set up a computer school in Soweto. We set up a second program at the Ethembeni School for disabled children near Durban. Over the years, about 150 Achilles South African members have participated in the New York City Marathon.

The Japanese chapter often sends nearly two dozen members to New York each year. Most are visually impaired. One year, I went to Japan to celebrate their 10th anniversary and ran with one of their athletes who is blind and has cerebral palsy. We gave her a handcycle and the following year, with four guides, she completed the New York City Marathon.

Over time, our micro community has grown organically in both size and scope, as our organizations have worked more extensively together. The initial test work we've done with children on the autism spectrum to engage them in Achilles and the difference that's made for their behavioral and academic outcomes is another example of how we are extending well beyond our original mission. We see positive indicators here, but we also realize there is an enormous opportunity to expand and build on our insights through new research, support and programs.

We have a clear vision, we've created a strategy and a plan of action to get there, we've found talented partners, and now we're executing the plan. Along the way we are continually making adjustments to overcome any challenges, funding our efforts and always looking for ways to extend our vision with new opportunities.

Whether it's new chapters in Philadelphia, Florida or New Zealand, every time we expand and grow, the entire Cigna organization is on board. This comes back to a company living its mission without having the need to run banner ads or skywrite its identity.

There are mission-based companies that are either nonprofit – so they're not performance-based publicly traded – or they're smaller scale. There are also performance-based nonprofits and public companies perceived to be less mission-oriented, albeit with missions.

From David: Community Impact

In 2016, Cigna took a big step toward helping curb the country's opioid epidemic, pledging to cut the use of those drugs among our customers by 25 percent over three years. Moreover, we set out to contribute to a national dialogue on the subject.

As I look back, I recognize we had no "right" to enter that space; we didn't prescribe or regulate opioids. But I was angry and said, "We're poisoning our society, but not enough people are talking about it." We had to act and we did.

We could have sat back and simply observed the crisis. We could have planned to get involved "one day." But we chose another path. We chose to go beyond traditional expectations to make broader, perhaps unexpected contributions to our customers, and to society.

Consistent with the tenets of our recipe, reducing opioid use was our vision. To create the right strategy, we convened a micro community of stakeholders – patients, physicians and other health care providers, pharmaceutical manufacturers and distributors, payers, pharmacists and governments – to determine where we were uniquely qualified to infuse "greater good" and act to reduce opioid use.

We tapped into our extensive experience with prevention, wellness and chronic disease management programs. We collaborated with the American Society of Addiction Medicine to provide customer claims data, in order to test and validate performance measures related to addiction treatment. We also encouraged the rapid adoption of the new Centers for Disease Control and Prevention guidelines on opioid use, and limited the quantity of opioids through exploring additional controls for high-risk customers. We also secured commitment of approximately 65,000 physicians to reduce the number of opioid prescriptions and treat substance use disorders as chronic diseases.

The Cigna Foundation provided one of its World of Difference grants to Shatterproof, a nonprofit organization committed to ending addiction, and contributed to the funding of naloxone – a life-saving drug that reverses the effects of a drug overdose. Cigna also began working with Stamp Out Stigma, an initiative spearheaded by the Association for Behavioral Health and Wellness, to change perceptions and reduce the stigma of mental illness and substance use.

We recognized we could bring together like-minded individuals in public forums to bring greater societal awareness to the epidemic, and to publicly explore opportunities for improvement. So, early on, Cigna sponsored a Washington Post forum, "Addiction in America," where a panel of civic and community leaders agreed that the continued failure to address opioid addiction would constitute nothing less than a national failure. In fact, we sponsored a variety of discussions such as this one around the United States, which I'm proud to say kick-started additional dialogue among local community leaders.

We achieved our 25 percent reduction target a full year ahead of our goal. By leveraging the power of the recipe and the micro communities we've convened, we've contributed to positive outcomes around a serious issue, but recognize there remains considerable work to do.

At Cigna, we've set our expectations internally, not by simply stating them but by living and doing it. By walking the walk with Achilles. Because too many times the words happen, but there's no music behind it or it seems to be superficial.

We are a mission-based company focused on changing people's lives for the better, and we acknowledge the demonstrable impact we can have on the communities we serve. We co-exist as a performance-based, publicly traded company, and we make no apology for that.

Similar to what some have said about the opioid crisis, some people have argued that the Achilles partnership was not in Cigna's space because it was not consistent with our for-profit mission. We disagree because this is about improving the health and well-being of individuals; we are committed to a sustainable partnership rather than episodic involvement.

Once you define your vision, visualize the path you want to take to strategize how it's going to happen and be open to all of the unique ways you can reach your goal with the like-minded people dedicated to making it happen.

Understand that your journey may go beyond your initial strategy. The vision is important, of course. But ensuring your success may require you to develop a broader and more diverse set of skills for better management of your micro community and to connect with the right talent.

Finally, take charge and communicate your vision, be active and get involved in every aspect of the recipe to guarantee success.

From Dick: A Source of Joy

January 9, 1983: The Achilles Track Club is established. Taking its name from the greatest warrior in Homer's epic tale "The Iliad", the organization is a source of inspiration for people with disabilities. Now known as Achilles International, its members are spirited competitors, passionate and highly supportive on one another. A reflection of the man behind its mission.

A "flag bearer for disabled runners" is how one writer characterized me. Impassioned bordering on obsessive. I wanted to pass on the same joy I felt when crossing the finish line at the 1976 New York City Marathon. I wanted to mainstream our members so they can assimilate and not be perceived as just one-legged people running. That driving force led to the creation of an international phenomenon, the true definition of the words rise up. Achilles is passion.

Nowhere is this better defined than in the stories about Achilles' own warriors, enjoying every weekend on running courses around the world.

Someone once asked me to reflect on what exactly Achilles does.

First, we encourage people with all types of disabilities to participate in mainstream athletics, running with people not necessarily disabled. This creates an awareness of disabled individuals and others begin to see them in a different light. They realize that people with disabilities can be athletes, competitors, leaders and teachers, and they can aspire to be productive members of society. This mainstreaming dynamic improves the comfort level on both sides – whether it's competing in an athletic event, meeting for a job interview, going on a date or enjoying a meal at a restaurant.

Second, when a person with a disability finishes their first marathon, it's typically an activity they never considered or even dreamed about. The achievement profoundly increases their sense of self. They think, "If I can achieve this, what else can be accomplished?" It could be anything, from going back to school to getting a job or seeking a promotion. Individual achievement also creates what I call a "halo." People perceive you not as an amputee simply trying to cross the street but as someone with star status. The way you are perceived increases your ability to succeed in every measure of your life. Most important is the way you perceive yourself. You are proud and confident.

Third, success helps change one's outlook from "What can I do for myself?" to "What can I do for others?" When you succeed, you learn the value of sharing your treasure. You become a giver and also learn valuable lessons: the great power of the group, being a group member and sharing the group's aspirations; the great power of setting goals and achieving them; and, of course, the great joy of love and friendship.

This is what defines Achilles, and it's what motivates us every day.

With chapters and members in over 95 locations within the United States and abroad, Achilles inspires members with specialized programs for children, teens, adults and veterans.

Some of our international stories are fantastic examples of micro communities in action. Each year, members of our Freedom Team travel to Columbia in conjunction with the U.S. State Department. They bring along prosthetics for the Columbian chapter members and they race and bond. There are also eight cities represented in New Zealand, thanks to Cigna.

Achilles continues to define the power of a true micro community. Its mission is simple yet always encourages people to do more. Coax the most out of an individual. It's an organization for every disabled person who ever dreamed of turning a first step into a lap around a gymnasium, a quarter of a mile, a 10K run and a marathon. A source of joy for everyone involved: members, volunteers, spectators and funding organizations. Achilles is a source of passion for individuals and those who support them. Their characters uplifted, their spirits soaring through the power of a collective achievement.

"We make a living by what we get. We make a life by what we give," Winston Churchill once said. The spirit of achievement through a motivated community of givers is well established in Achilles, now well into its fourth decade. From Australia to South Africa, Germany to Peru, members and volunteers are there. Supporting. Encouraging. Emboldening the spirit. Celebrating at the finish line.

The Cigna/Achilles partnership reinforces the power of the individual, knowing that every individual is unique. Everything in our universe revolves around the individual. We have various sustainable micro communities all focused on helping people by applying our Cigna/Achilles recipe.

The essence of a micro community continually inspiring new micro communities, extending, growing and focusing an individual is what David and I like to call the power of possibilities. This theory puts the individual at the center of our universe and everything we do is focused around creating new micro communities to help individuals achieve their goals.

So, the individual becomes the incentive, the reason for delivering results.

Ultimately, there are multiple micro communities because this is not a monolithic approach. A recipe is applied and it is individual, humanistic, goal-oriented, supportive and helping when people fall figuratively and literally in pursuit of their goal. We keep fueling those goals because, if we can inspire the individual with a sense of purpose and an aspiration, a lot of good things will happen.

Dick Traum
with New
York City
Chapter
athletes

Marcia
Monaco at
the half
way point
at the New
York City
Marathon

04

MIXING IT
ALL TOGETHER

"What you want to ignite in others
must first burn inside yourself."

– Charlotte Brontë

Zoe Koplowitz was diagnosed with multiple sclerosis at age 25. Based on the medical advice common 40-plus years ago regarding MS, including reducing stress and avoiding strenuous activity, her physicians told her to avoid exercise for fear of worsening her MS symptoms. But after choking on a vitamin pill and almost dying, she committed to make a change in her life. She threw caution to the wind and set a long-term goal to run a marathon.

Focused on accomplishing her goal, Zoe attended a workout with Achilles and completed a half-mile walk that evening. She continued her training to increase her capacity and prepare for longer events. At the same time, she saw significantly slower declines in her physical well-being. While remarkable at the time, subsequent studies of living and exercising with MS have shown that participants spoke of a positive reversal in physical function, which has far-reaching implications for multiple aspects of their lives, including their psychological outlook, sense of independence, overcoming isolation and their relationship with their spouse.

Zoe was empowered and inspired by her own success and went on to complete her first marathon, taking nearly 20 hours and finishing last. Still, her heightened confidence and spirit of achievement was powerful. Her sequel was even more impactful.

As she continued on Fourth Avenue while running her second marathon (at this point in first place because she had started much earlier than the main pack of runners), Zoe heard someone shout, "Are you Grete Waitz?" Yes, she had endured discomfort throughout the course, but was far from being the Norwegian marathon runner and former world record holder. Not surprisingly, Zoe was flattered and smiled broadly. Yet in true fashion, she kept her unfailing sense of humor. The following year, her T-shirt was emblazoned with "I'm not Grete!" Zoe eventually completed over 20 marathons.

"She threw caution to the wind and set a long-term goal to run a marathon."

PROFILES IN COURAGE

Zoe Koplowitz

Achilles Marathoner | Florida

At 40, I was determined to get back everything I had lost to MS over the years. I decided that running a marathon was going to be my goal. I had a vision of myself launching across the finish line without any appliances, wearing a designer tracksuit. In reality, I would likely fall on my face every five feet!

I needed to find a vehicle to help me achieve my goal. I called the New York Roadrunners Club and told them of my disability and my desire to run a marathon, and they told me about Achilles.

At that point, I had no experience with the disabled community and no idea how to run the distance. Dick Traum took me out on the first night and after our run, he said to me, "I can see you're overwhelmed. So you'll come back again and again." And he was right. I was overwhelmed, yet it was also exhilarating. I knew how important it was to invent my concept of winning and how it's not always about finishing first. It's about doing what you do from the center of your being with everything you've got. That's what makes a winner.

I still get a little misty when I think about finishing my first race hours later, after everybody had long gone. By the time I finished there was no hot chocolate, no bagels, no T-shirts, nothing. But I had been given a gift that no one could ever take from me.

> In that moment, I realized that I had the ability to go the distance, whether it was on the road or in a race or just in my life, every day.

That's the essential lesson that I pass on to other people.

As I wrote in my book, *The Winning Spirit: Life Lessons Learned in Last Place*, if I was going to live with this thing called MS, then I was going to make it matter. I never thought I would become an author and public speaker, and I never imagined the notoriety that would come with it, including being in a "Got Milk" ad that was photographed by Annie Leibovitz and featured in a L'eggs Pantyhose ad. I took the learnings from my journey as a student and transitioned into becoming the teacher. That was my purpose. I really believe that everybody has a purpose in the world. Mine is to contribute to the greater good. I'm one of those "pay it forward" people, and I thoroughly believe in that.

A marathon is both a metaphor and a race. Many people who are struggling and disabled will never complete a marathon. But everybody does their own marathon in one way or another. For some people, just getting their clothes on in the morning and getting set up for their day, that's their marathon. We all need to give ourselves the finishers' medals that we deserve. For me, Achilles has been about friendships and the realization that there are no limitations to what you can do.

Even with the onset of diabetes and kidney failure, Zoe has made it her mission to help others with MS realize their dreams of becoming marathon runners. As she passes her skills on to others, Zoe the receiver has become Zoe the giver, learning to acting and then mentoring others.

Zoe has become a legend among Achilles members and is one of our most devoted ambassadors. For some time, she was speaking to high school students about overcoming obstacles, and how a disability should not interfere with your life. Following her speeches and the typical standing ovations, each student was given a deck of Achilles playing cards with the picture of an athlete on the front and, on the back, a description of the disability he or she overcame. Typically, the students lined up for as long as it took to get Zoe's autograph on her card.

Like Zoe, many Achilles members who have redefined their sense of self through personal achievement have a propensity to actively seek out and inspire others, becoming active mentors for the formation of new micro communities.

This spirit of exceeding expectations – leveraging your reach beyond your initial objectives – lies at the heart and soul of everyone who accomplishes a goal and then unselfishly helps others to define and realize their goals. The basic model for this dynamic comes from the world of medicine.

The traditional method for physicians in surgical training is known as "see one, do one, teach one." The basis of this teaching method is formed from the basic stages of learning, mentoring and imitating behavior to accelerate development. As a result, new attending physicians are well-prepared to supervise their own teams of medical students and residents.

Achilles has taken this concept and applied it to a three-part model of learning, acting and mentoring others.

- **Learning.** Within micro communities, individuals observe others with their same perceived limitations performing in mainstream environments. They immediately see the impact of a changed behavior and envision reaching a similar goal. Dick saw this when Zoe first attended an Achilles meeting and took her initial steps to complete a half-mile.

- **Acting.** Next, they are encouraged and empowered to take on a new challenge or activity, in our case to participate in running events. A community of like-minded people provides the programs and tools to motivate and support individuals as they take action, modeling the desired behavior. The individuals continually revise and broaden the scope of their strategy – referring back to the touchstones of the vision along the way. Zoe's success as a marathoner improved her self-confidence and her spirit of achievement.

- **Mentoring.** Then they are inspired by their own achievement and seek new ways to unselfishly pass their successes on to others – developing and increasing the passion and commitment across more micro communities. Indeed, the events where Zoe spoke to high school students became micro communities in and of themselves.

When David guided Stefan LeRoy along with his ultra-marathoner friend Caitlin in the 2018 Boston Marathon, the three of them formed our own situational micro community.

At the mile 24 mark, Caitlin said to David, "I learned a lot from you today."

That felt incredibly rewarding. This particular, situational micro community will probably never convene again. But during that time, David was able to give Caitlin all that he had learned over the last seven years guiding runners such as Stefan. Even though she never served as a guide over a marathon distance before, she came to understand and appreciate techniques and little tricks to ensure a successful outcome.

Caitlin the receiver had become Caitlin the giver – fully prepared to now create her own situational micro community, following the model to share her newfound skills and mentor others.

Zoe's and Caitlin's stories serve as reminders of how we can leverage the power of micro communities to inspire and encourage others to become givers and mentors. Zoe started as a receiver and evolved into being a giver by asking, "What's next?" Caitlin is on her way to mentoring others. Through simple learning principles – including experience, observation, action and deliberate practice – the students have become the teachers.

The receivers have become the givers.

Another example is Richard Bernstein, who began as a blind non-athlete searching for his identity. Richard joined Achilles and started competing in short races, then marathons and, ultimately, became a triathlete and a celebrated Ironman. Still, that level of achievement wasn't enough and Richard asked, "What's next?" He became an attorney in the state of Michigan and then ultimately rose to the level of Supreme Court justice – The Honorable Richard Bernstein!

The "Learning. Acting. Mentoring." model inspires those in the Achilles micro community to motivate others and take action. As we pass on our skills, we see a multiplier effect spawning new micro communities of receivers who become givers.

The Potential Rewards are Limitless

2018 Boston Marathon

These stories we just shared highlight the key ingredients of our simple recipe and demonstrate the power of micro communities.

The ChildObesity180 initiative proved to us how the process for setting clear objectives and taking the steps to achieve them begins with establishing the vision and guides everyone on the journey. This micro community asked itself, "What do we want to achieve?" Then it defined, communicated and acted on the vision, effectively integrating the mission of a nonprofit organization into the culture of a for-profit corporation.

Achilles athletes such as Alfredo De Los Santos and Tom Davis remind us of how a clear strategy can help us to achieve our vision. When we build a solid action plan into the strategy, we set the bar and create a sense of purpose to get the hard work done. Achilles Kids was a micro community borne from Terry Fox's legacy and inspiration, reminding us how the right plan and the mindset of a motivated micro community can help us achieve our vision.

Achilles Kids is also an excellent example of how we can draw from myriad resources – be they human or financial – to build an infrastructure, get programs off the ground and sustain them over the long term. Achilles volunteers and trainers make sure young athletes such as Tyler McNeil have everything they need to overcome their disabilities, find their true identity and get to the finish line. Coupled with research and funding from the Cigna Foundation, dedicated resources like these support the vision and strategy of our micro community.

For Stefan LeRoy, the difference between success and failure was his ability to execute his plan for success. When he made his case to run the Boston Marathon, there was no turning back, and we had to do whatever it took to help him and achieve his goal.

Matias Ferreira had a seemingly impossible goal, but his strategy was unwavering and he was determined to overcome obstacles and make adjustments to make his vision a reality. Willpower alone is never enough. We need to encourage frequent and honest feedback, trust the plan and be tenacious enough to adjust to anything that stands between us and our vision.

Cigna's steps to address and help curb the country's opioid epidemic shows us how a situational micro community – built around the energy and sheer fortitude to make a profound change – can broaden and expand on the vision across a more sustainable enterprise. As we write this, Cigna is now seeking to bring similar focus to the loneliness epidemic in the United States.

Whether you want to run (as we focused on here), learn a language, study an instrument, establish a charity or pursue countless other ambitions, your aspiration – whether large or small – is certainly doable. Define it. Set a goal to do something extraordinary or help someone set their aspirational goal and imagine achieving it. Then, make the vision an integral part of your life. It can either be a simple objective or something unusual and seemingly unattainable – and yet either way it's well within the realm of reality. It all begins with you.

David Cordani running with Matias Ferreira

2018 Boston Marathon

THE COURAGE TO GO FORWARD

EPILOGUE

"Setting an example is not the main means of influencing others, it is the only means."

– Albert Einstein

courage

noun \ cour·age

1. the quality of mind or spirit that enables a person to face difficulty, danger, pain, etc., without fear; bravery.

2. Obsolete. the heart as the source of emotion.

Idioms

3. have the courage of one's convictions, to act in accordance with one's beliefs, especially in spite of criticism.

From David:

We have been so fortunate and inspired to witness the courage and determination of others – their tenacity and willpower have been uplifting and heartening.

For us, doing good for others is not a duty, it is a joy because it helps them rise beyond any perceived limitation and also increases our own health and happiness.

With this in mind, let's revisit considerations we raised in the Prologue.

Have you ever wondered what you can do to change a person's life?

We have seen the power of possibilities – the power we have to change a life – and we see lives changing for the better every day because of the concepts addressed in this book. Most of the time, the challenge is a deceptively simple one. For example, someone decides to pursue a goal such as learning to ride a bike or taking piano lessons. Sometimes the goal is more significant and less tangible, such as struggling with a perceived limitation like loneliness or a physical disability.

Our one-on-one interactions, including co-existing with others as Cigna has learned through its studies on loneliness, can realize enormous potential in an individual's life by uplifting and encouraging them to visualize their achievement or their heightened sense of well-being.

You take a walk, have coffee and talk about the challenge or goal. You introduce that person or yourself to an individual or group of people achieving or overcoming an obstacle, you see the results and realize there is a path and a recipe to achieve your goal or overcome your challenge.

I remember a Navy admiral telling me about his experience visiting veterans at Walter Reed. He said, "Sometimes I just sit down and I listen. You have no idea how valuable that is." It may sound simple and trite, but the art of listening is something we believe can also be taken for granted.

As the Greek philosopher Diogenes said, "We have two ears and only one tongue in order that we may hear more and speak less." Oftentimes, texting back and forth with Matias didn't always work well for us. Our live conversations were noteworthy because it was important to just be there and, most importantly, to listen. Sometimes listening without judgment or expectations can make a big difference in someone's life. Quietly observing and acknowledging others' thoughts and concerns can be more important than anything we can ever say.

Have you ever wondered how things that seemingly feel impossible can become possible?

We have seen individuals go beyond seemingly impossible goals, accomplish incredible tasks and, in turn, inspire others. When Cedric King faced what looked like an impossible marathon in horrific conditions, his micro community picked him up and set him back on course. He continues to complete marathons and now motivates others as a sought-after speaker, inspiring them to take control of their lives and follow their dreams.

Trisha Meili overcame tremendous odds, competed in mainstream running events and went on to inspire others through public speaking engagements, her work on the Achilles board and the annual Hope & Possibility Race. Trisha and Cedric are living proof of how the power of a motivated micro community can inspire someone to find their way back to society and go beyond any perceived limitations.

An injury from military duty can be demoralizing and life-shattering. But members of the Achilles Freedom Team are out there proving how determination trumps setbacks and insecurities every day. As Alfredo De Los Santos, Tom Davis and Stefan LeRoy have proven, the encouragement they received from our micro community served as the foundation for their return to a more normalized life. Mainstreaming with non-disabled runners gave them a reason to get up in the morning, view their lives as meaningful and valuable and overcome seemingly impossible obstacles.

Have you ever wondered how – without having a large infrastructure or organization – individuals are able to accomplish great things?

Like a stone tossed into a pond, sometimes our smallest efforts can send out ripples that resonate into larger more sustainable endeavors.

When I first attended the Walt Disney World Half Marathon, I was simply there to support the participants. It was equally important to keep everyone engaged. I knew Dick would be there, and I wanted to show my respect for him and Achilles. Little did I know that I would walk away inspired to do as much as I could, to become a guide and move the Cigna/Achilles partnership forward. I also realized that this didn't require great financial backing or large resources to make it happen.

Family, community and achievement – these are the fundamental components of the partnership we have created, this is the pebble we have tossed and what drives our micro community. Together, we have drawn on this dynamic to influence the lives of others.

Through our experiences, we know that anything is achievable if you're willing to go after your goals in a disciplined way. Further, the probability of achieving your objectives increases exponentially when you join like-minded people who know the road map, share your vision and take the steps to make dreams a reality.

We all know the old philanthropy orientation of "You give a little time or you write a check." This is not about giving a little time or writing a check. This is about putting your heart into something and bonding with others to leverage what we like to call a "multiplier effect" of like-minded and passionate people.

On a more personal note, both of us believe we have a responsibility to make a difference in the communities where we work, serve and play. It doesn't have to be hard. Take Cigna's mission as an example: to improve the health, well-being and sense of security of the people we serve. If you can't find something that is of personal interest to you that fits in health, well-being and sense of security in your communities, then you're not looking hard enough.

In the words of author and speaker Brené Brown, "You can choose courage, or you can choose comfort, but you cannot choose both."

Too often, because of the fast-paced lives we live, we have a propensity to fall into a category of "Yeah, I want to do that. I want to do that someday." And if you can tap into that discretionary goodness of your own inner human will – and gather the courage to take the first step – you can make it happen.

> *When I run races such as the Boston Marathon with Stefan, we typically don't run by many people early on. At the start, dozens of mobility-impaired people take off and everybody else passes us. The wheelchairs pass. The handcycles pass. The professionals wisp by. All the able-bodied athletes pass.*

> *But then, in the last five miles, we start passing people. And it happens every time. People look at us like, "Holy shit." And you see other runners lift up their energy because they are witnessing something incredible.*

> *So, take that first step to realizing your aspirations. Let your own spirit and sense of achievement inspire and propel you into the future. One year from now, you could be looking back with the same sense of joy and achievement.*

> *So, let's – all of us – walk the talk.*

David Cordani

From Dick:

Life always tells us to set the bar higher and go faster. From the start, our families have always encouraged us to meet and exceed the bar, bound by their energy, determination and passion to encourage every member.

Failure is not an option.

> *Finishing my first marathon was a turning point in my life and is an accomplishment that meant the world to me. But as I've grown older, affiliation has surpassed achievement as the motivating force in my life. My work with Achilles has been life-altering not only for me, but also for everyone involved in the program. I am touched by the impact we have been able to make on individuals' lives, and I cannot wait to tackle the next challenges. It's not just about my achievements as a marathoner, I work every day to help other athletes have this same life-changing experience. This organization is nothing short of extraordinary, and I am immeasurably proud of my affiliation with it.*
>
> *My view of the future is to encourage research; expand the number of chapters and integrate them with our Hope & Possibility Race; dramatically increase the scope of Achilles Kids; and work out a method of increasing the use of handcycles.*
>
> *And I wonder how many more marathons are ahead of me.*
>
> *Wish me luck!*

Dick Traum

The Cigna/Achilles partnership encapsulates a vision of human togetherness, the bond of a family guided by its efforts to combat uncertainty and doubt, to encourage and to rebuild self-confidence among the individuals we serve. Although we have taken great strides in the four decades that have passed since Dick first started his journey to help disabled individuals become runners, much remains to be done. Yet dedicated solutions can only be pursued when we collectively answer the question: "What do we want to achieve?"

For-profit corporations frequently have funding resources and means to make monetary commitments. This can never be enough. These organizations also need to draw from their motivated employees to answer the call. This requires effective leadership with the intelligence, sagacity and skill to galvanize others, define the vision and see the mission through.

On the nonprofit side, altruistic endeavors alone cannot sustain themselves without impassioned partners, volunteers and members. Strong leadership with a strong sense of purpose to help others – whether it's finding health or personal healing or reaching a goal – is also essential to remaining true to the vision and the spirit of unselfishly serving others.

Beyond leadership, there are givers and there are receivers. Many times, we have seen the receivers transform and then give selflessly to others. This dynamic heartens and inspires us to continue our mission indefinitely. Because we realize there is a benefit for all, from the veteran returning from battle realizing that he can become a productive member of society to the volunteer determined to make a difference in the life of a child with autism. When we pledge to improve the lives of others, we often improve our own.

Do you need more inspiration? Join us at a Cigna/Achilles event. You will witness an outpouring of love, friendship and support that defines our micro community and our successful partnership.

Acknowledgments

First, we want to thank you, our readers. You are the reason we decided to bring this book to life. So, once again, thank you for your interest in exploring our unique partnership and experiences.

We also want to thank everyone who has selflessly committed to helping someone else achieve their goals.

To bring this book to fruition, we created our own micro community of talented people and we are grateful to all of them. We especially want to acknowledge the Cigna and Achilles teams who helped make this book a reality, including Lisa Bacus, Chris Stenrud and Phil Mann from Cigna, and Janet Patton, Karen Lewis and Larry Sillen from Achilles.

When our vision went to the manuscript stage, several people made sure we executed. Marty Galasso helped us to organize our thoughts and ideas, and a number of people at Edelman Public Relations shared many ideas that were incorporated into this book. So, thank you Jackie Kahn, Dan Santow, Melinda Boisjolie, Brian Roy, Lisa Parisi and Josey Feltes.

To our families, thank you for giving us advice and encouragement to achieve beyond anything we could imagine. You are as important to this book getting written as anyone.

David also wants to thank his wife, Sherry, children Caroline and Nicholas, and his more than 45,000 Cigna colleagues around the world who work every day to embody the company's mission of improving the health, well-being and sense of security of those it serves.

Dick especially wants to thank his wife, Elizabeth, son, Joe, daughter-in-law, Josie, and granddaughter, Bella.

Thanks to the Morgan James Publishing team for helping us bring the book to market.

CPSIA information can be obtained
at www.ICGtesting.com
Printed in the USA
BVHW09*1426110818
523989BV00002B/2/P